"The secret to a great customer (employee experience (EX). In other words, what's happening on the inside of an organization is going to be felt on the outside by the customer. Jason Bradshaw knows this firsthand, as that was one of his responsibilities in his role as an executive at a major brand, and now he teaches you. Don't just read this book. Use this book. Execute the ideas on these pages, and you will positively impact the experience you create for both your employees and your customers."

—SHEP HYKEN, CUSTOMER SERVICE EXPERT
AND *NEW YORK TIMES* BEST-SELLING AUTHOR
OF *THE AMAZEMENT REVOLUTION*

"It's simple: customer experience matters now, more than ever, and in this book, Jason will help you accelerate improvements."

—JEANNE BLISS, COFOUNDER OF CUSTOMER
EXPERIENCE PROFESSIONALS ASSOCIATION AND
FOUNDER AND PRESIDENT OF CUSTOMERBLISS.COM

"It's All About CEX isn't just any customer experience book, it provides the keys to make lifetime advocates of customers and employees. Bradshaw provides strategies that you can implement in every level of your company that will deliver immediate results and make you famous."

—JOE CALLOWAY, BEST-SELLING AUTHOR OF
BECOMING A CATEGORY OF ONE AND MEMBER OF
THE PROFESSIONAL SPEAKERS HALL OF FAME

"*It's All About CEX* is a masterfully crafted, insightful resource for anyone who seeks to drive customer loyalty and referrals. Written from wisdom, experience, and a deep understanding of how to drive a branded customer experience, *It's All About CEX* is refreshing, approachable, and empowering! It is filled with actionable tools that will drive sustainable customer success!"

—JOSEPH MICHELLI, NEW YORK TIMES NUMBER-ONE BEST-SELLING AUTHOR OF BOOKS LIKE *DRIVEN TO DELIGHT*, *LEADING THE STARBUCKS WAY*, AND *THE NEW GOLD STANDARD*

"Bradshaw's book absolutely nails it! He takes us on a journey that explains why both customer and employee experience matters so significantly—and he provides real-world strategies you can implement today to create lifelong customers and advocates. Apply his advice and become iconic for your outstanding customer experiences. This is a must-read!"

—SCOTT MCKAIN, GLOBAL THOUGHT-LEADER ON CREATING DISTINCTION IN BUSINESS AND AUTHOR OF MULTIPLE BEST-SELLING BOOKS INCLUDING *7 TENETS OF TAXI TERRY* AND *WHAT CUSTOMERS REALLY WANT*

IT'S ALL ABOUT CEX!

IT'S ALL ABOUT

The Essential Guide to
Customer & Employee Experience

———

JASON S. BRADSHAW

LIONCREST
PUBLISHING

IT'S ALL ABOUT CEX!

The Essential Guide to Customer and Employee Experience

ISBN   978-1-5445-1244-0 *Hardcover*

      978-1-5445-1242-6 *Paperback*

      978-1-5445-1243-3 *Ebook*

CONTENTS

INTRODUCTION

MY JOURNEY TO EXPERIENCE

My parents, David and Nicola, had a profound influence on me, an influence that ultimately inspired me to start my own business at the ripe old age of fourteen. I was born in an Australian country town called Murgon, which, at the time, had a population of two thousand.

As I was growing up, my parents always had a side hustle— some business they worked on outside of their normal jobs. My grandparents also ran their own independent clothing and drapery retail company. During holidays, I could often be found at either my parents' or my grandparents' businesses, not only observing them at work but, whenever possible, also engaging with them and trying to learn. I was encouraged to ask questions about what was happening so I could understand what was going on.

I had many opportunities to spend time with my father and mother in their various professional and business pursuits. I pursued many of my own projects as well. For example, I used to bottle, label, and sell gun oil. One of my father's lifelong side hustles was gunsmithing. So a few times a year, we traveled to firearms shows where he would buy, sell, and trade associated items. When I was a teenager, he always reserved space on his table at these shows so I could sell some of my bottles of oil.

My mother had her own side hustles, and at one point in her career, she was part owner of an auctioneering business. On weekends, I traveled with her to rural auctions to help with various tasks, including record keeping and running auction sheets for auctioneers.

Each of these opportunities taught me how to get things done and, as will become clear throughout this book, instilled in me a bias for building momentum using customer and employee experience. I learned early on that experience is the key differentiator of a successful business.

Seeing both my parents and grandparents run their own businesses piqued my interest, so I began, even as a child, to read business magazines. I started with *Australian Small Business and Investing*, which I would ask my father to buy for me every month. It was filled with articles about entrepreneurs, but I was particularly fascinated by the various business opportunities presented in the classified ads.

At thirteen, I made my first Amazon.com purchase, which was a big deal at the time. Remember that Amazon only officially came to Australia in 2018, but I started using it long before that. My first purchase was a Tom Peters book called *The Pursuit of WOW!* on a twin cassette tape (which shows my age). In the book, Peters talks about wowing both customers and employees in order to grow. I find it interesting that he was talking about this back in 1994, and here we are, in 2018, still talking about the importance of experience in making an organization sustainable and successful.

MY FIRST BUSINESS: TENACITY AND SERVICE

My desire to read and learn about the world exposed me to small-business concepts, so by the age of fourteen, I was ready to start my own business. To be honest, my primary interest wasn't becoming an entrepreneur—I saw it as a means to an end. Chiefly, I wanted to own the latest and greatest gadgets, whether my parents could afford them or not. My parents provided me with a great upbringing and supported me in every way, but there was one thing they wouldn't freely buy me: the latest and greatest computer tech or gadget of the season.

I came up with a harebrained idea. If I could get some-one to sell me computers at wholesale prices, I could turn around and sell them for a profit, and with that money, I could fund my desire for the latest computer tech. This was the heyday of Gateway computers, when desktop computers were much bigger than they are today (and could do much less than the phones we carry in our pock-ets). At that time, a cutting-edge computer cost well over $4,000, and I had to have one!

By then, my family and I lived in a regional Australian town called Toowoomba, the largest noncapital inland city at the time, with a population somewhere between ninety thousand and a hundred thousand. I figured I could ship computers in from the closest major city, so I began contacting businesses in Brisbane to find a supplier. I also began looking for customers, talking to friends of my parents, neighbors, and anyone else I came into contact with. Through that experience, I learned the importance of both tenacity and customer service, les-sons that have served me well ever since.

After choosing a business name, filling out all the paper-work to register the business, and sending it off to the government, I went to the bank to open a checking account. The bank informed me that at fourteen, I was legally too young to open an account. This created a major hurdle because in 1994, a checking account was the only way for businesses to transact.

I could have given up at that point, but it became a teachable moment. Rather than accept the bank's rejection, I tracked down the actual legislation to see what the law said. In doing so, I discovered that the law didn't technically forbid a fourteen-year-old from opening a checking account. As I recall, it said, in essence, "An individual must show that they have the mental capacity to use a checking account."

With this information in hand, I sat down at my typewriter—because I didn't have my dream computer yet—and promptly wrote the bank a long letter. In it, I explained why I believed the bank was in error and how I met the requirements of the law by the simple fact that I had successfully registered a business. Upon receiving my letter, with a little more pushing from me, the bank agreed and allowed me to open an account.

Now that I had a checking account and a business name, I started setting up suppliers. All of the suppliers were cash on delivery, so everything was built to order and shipped on payment. In the business world, people talk about the importance of cash flow. In my first business, it was *everything*. If I didn't get paid by my customers in advance, I couldn't afford to purchase the product from my suppliers.

Through all of this, my tenacity paid off. A large painting-supply business in Toowoomba asked me to provide a computer retail and wholesale solution with a complete accounting software suite for their brand-new retail facility. I put together a quote for the hardware and accounting software. At the time, I knew nothing about accounting software, so I had to identify the best software, engage a Queensland distributor, and convince them to contract with me as their local reseller. In the end, at fourteen years old, I supplied the painting-supply company with brand-new computer hardware and the accounting software they needed to run their multimillion-dollar business.

I soon began to generate positive press. I was interviewed by *Australian Small Business and Investing*, the magazine that had first fueled my desire to start a business. During the interview, I was asked what made me different from every other computer business, and I responded that my level of service set me apart. I couldn't play on price. I wasn't the cheapest, but I delivered a top-notch service experience that customers wanted to talk about and were prepared to pay for.

This commitment to customer service enabled me to expand the business to other products. People don't buy a new computer every month, so I needed new revenue streams. My plan was to sell complementary products. People who buy computers need things such as printer paper, ink cartridges, blank disks, and other office supplies, so I began to offer them. I also sold mobile phones, telephone systems, fax machines, and a whole range of office equipment. This allowed me to build a stable customer base by creating ongoing relationships that strengthened my reputation and helped me grow.

Of course, this first business wasn't going to take over the world of office equipment. That wasn't my intention. I only wanted to make enough money to buy the latest shiny gadgets, but I had loyal customers who were happy to refer me to others.

Those loyal customers funded my hobbies and then some. In addition to earning a nice amount of money, I'd started building lifetime skills in sales, negotiations, operations, and of course, how customer experience (CX) can be a differentiator that grows your business.

As I said, I couldn't offer the best prices. For example, one of my regular products was a permanent marker, but I couldn't buy it wholesale. Instead, I simply bought them in bulk from other retailers, put a margin on each one, and sold them to my clients. While the margin wasn't high, it still made my prices slightly higher than most major suppliers. Still, my customers needed permanent markers, so they bought them often. With each sale, I had another opportunity to continue my relationship with them, acting as a direct supplier of their office needs in a way that was convenient for them. You see, sometimes it's not about squeezing the most profit out of a product; it's about continuing the customer relationship by providing more opportunities to offer a great experience and a needed product.

As a result of this first experience, I have remained committed to differentiating myself through service. Over the years, customer expectations have changed substantially. People expect a higher level of service from companies than they used to. Pure customer service is no longer the differentiator. Now you have to deliver an experience to both your employees and your customers.

Think about your own business and the experiences you deliver. Is there a way to increase the frequency of interactions with customers? Each interaction helps you build trust and create repeat and referral business.

MY SECOND BUSINESS: CREATING AN EXPERIENCE

When I got to college, I just wanted to be a kid again. During my first year, I lived on campus, went to parties, and put more focus on my social life than my academic life. This caused me to jettison my first business.

It didn't take long to realize that the party lifestyle wasn't sustainable—it certainly wasn't feeding my thirst for growth—so I got a job as an outbound telemarketer, selling carpet-cleaning and pest control services. As it happened, my mother worked for the same company but in a different capacity, so she recommended the job. Every day when I wasn't in class, I made cold calls for four to five hours a day. This experience taught me a different set of sales skills, but unfortunately, it didn't last long. By the time I was nineteen, the company had gone bankrupt.

I decided to start my own domestic and commercial cleaning company. Setup was easy because I had a number of displaced team members from the former company at my disposal. The business, which was called Ultra Clean, offered domestic and commercial cleaning along with pest control and general cleaning services. I subcontracted individuals to perform the work and set up a telemarketing team.

The business evolved over time. At one point, I turned my parents' lounge and dining room into a call center. At another point, I leased a shop front. Through it all, the focus remained on providing a higher level of customer care. I didn't push fire sales or aggressive sales tactics. Instead, I made sure my employees felt as if they were a part of a team and that our customers could see we genuinely cared about them and weren't after quick money.

By offering a wide range of services, we created long-term relationships with customers, and we always followed up with them. Anytime we provided a service, we called the customer afterward to thank them for their business. Then we followed the call with written communication, so they knew we cared and would be available when they needed us again. This was key to building loyalty and business quickly grew, as customers returned for additional services.

In my second business, I again learned a number of things that have served me throughout my career. First, I learned the importance of creating a strong team. In my first business, I had been the sole trader, so the only person who could get angry or become disengaged was me. If I was having a bad experience, it was my own fault. With my second business, I had a team of people whose performance and retention were largely dependent on the experience I created for them.

Our sales model was arguably one of the most difficult: cold-call outbound marketing. Callers had to interrupt unsuspecting people in order to offer them products and services they didn't necessarily want. We've all experienced getting an unexpected telemarketing call. A typical response is "Leave me alone," before hanging up. Let me tell you, it's not easy being on the other end of those calls.

Think about how you respond when a telemarketer calls

your house. Think about how quickly you get off the phone. The people making those calls endure a constant stream of negative reactions. It requires incredible tenacity to handle rejection after rejection, to keep reaching out and making those calls, working to make a sale. Many people despise telemarketers, and there's a whole industry of "do not call" registries and tools to block such calls.

I absolutely support a right to privacy, and if someone doesn't want to receive such calls, I support efforts to block them. Still, think about the strength and tenacity it takes to succeed as a telemarketer when there are so many roadblocks to making a sale. Whether B2B or B2C, it's one of the toughest gigs out there.

When someone is good at it, companies don't want to lose them. They possess an efficiency and effectiveness that new recruits, who are just learning the craft, lack. It was all the more important that I created a strong sense of employee engagement along with clear direction. I did this not by offering free lunches or incentive trips—we lacked the money for such things—but by humanizing my team members in everything they did. That meant giving them every tool and resource they needed to be successful, while also demonstrating that I was willing to do whatever it took to help the team.

For example, we won a commercial cleaning job at a manufacturing site that hadn't seen any cleaners in years. The workshop was so filthy that none of our contract cleaners wanted the job. Rather than forcing my employees to do it, I jumped in the car and drove to the customer's workshop myself. When employees see the founder of their organization scrubbing toilets in a place so filthy—it probably would have been easier to spray-bathe the whole facility in acid—it makes a big impact. This approach inspired the team to do the work in subsequent weeks, so it was a win-win.

We always worked through problems as a team. In one instance, we faced major tax legislation changes, so I created a slideshow, called everyone together, and walked them through the changes. I wanted to eliminate any fear they might be harboring while also ensuring that the business was meeting its obligations.

This was part of a broader focus on paying attention to small details. I worked hard to improve the day-to-day experience of our team, making things as simple and easy to understand as possible. As a leader, this meant constantly looking for ways to help team members. It didn't mean I gave them everything they wanted. Rather, I actively helped them achieve their goals.

The cleaning business is fierce, but in good times and bad, we had a strong core team that stuck together. Anyone with money can buy equipment and start cleaning carpets. You don't need a university degree to learn the business, so we had a lot of competition. However, creating a strong team that constantly looked out for our customers differentiated us from the rest of the market. We supported one another, we cared for our customers, and we achieved tremendous success as a result.

CREATING CONNECTIONS

After running my own businesses, I decided I wanted to try something different. I had already experienced being my own boss. Now I wanted to become part of an organization bigger than myself, so I started looking for part-time work at a large corporation. I studied numerous organizations and registered with recruitment agencies, and in no time, I got a job working in a call center at a large banking institution. I was quickly elevated to the position of assistant call-center manager, a promotion that came about in part because I was willing to take shifts no one else wanted.

This was my first foray into a big corporate call center. The call center I worked for was part of a special projects team, and at one point, the bank lost some large tenders, which forced them to downsize our team. As that was happening, I looked after my team, kept them informed, and made sure we were always transparent with them.

In 1999, the call center was closed, but my former team members still reach out to me from time to time. Ten years after the call center closed, a former employee called me and said, "I wish I was still working for you, because I still remember how you led." I had another employee at the call center whom I had to make redundant. Four years later, I wound up managing her at a different company, and I had to make her redundant again. Despite this, she remained positive about her experience under my leadership. Both of these examples reinforce the power of creating connections with your employees.

THE POWER OF EXPERIENCE

In every job I've had since then, I've always focused on two key areas. First, I look after the people within my sphere of influence, knowing that if I do, they will become a high-performing team and deliver results that reflect positively on the business. Second, I make sure to look after both internal and external customers.

Having a clear focus on these two things has enabled me to work effectively in banking and finance, telecommunications, government, and even healthcare. I sat on the board of a health promotion, services, and support not-for-profit company for seven years as chair of the finance and audit committee, and I discovered that you can focus on accounting and legislative compliance while still delivering an excellent employee and customer experience.

In every industry, the same holds true. I've worked for the Australian government's largest procurement organization. I've worked in retail, media, and the automotive industry. In every instance, I have been able to deliver exceptional improvements by focusing on the employee and customer experience. At one organization, I was able to deliver $60 million in savings while improving operational outcomes and revenue growth, reducing employee turnover, and increasing customers through this same focus.

WHAT YOU CAN EXPECT

In this book, we will explore the importance of experience. Businesses that have stood the test of time have been consistent and tenacious about delivering an experience to employees and customers. By doing so, they've been able to move and shape their business year after year because they make a difference in the lives of their team members and customers, and they impact the communities in which they work and serve. Specific examples we'll look at include organizations such as Southwest Airlines, Zappos, John Deere, Warby Parker, and Telstra.

As industries become more global and people become

more disconnected from their neighbors, the experiences we have with each other become more important than ever. We'll explore how that plays out in everything we do.

We will also look at the ways in which both employees and customers measure their experience with an organization and why it matters. If you give people what they're looking for, you start to get improved performance, repeat business, and referrals.

Finally, I will provide practical advice that you can start acting on now. This book doesn't offer a silver bullet. There's no single action that will suddenly fix all your customer or employee experience issues. You're not going to do one thing and immediately have a million fans raving about your business. Obviously, there are some tactical marketing activities that can get people raving about your business right away, but we're not talking about that here. Instead, we are talking about creating lifelong fans, and there are some actions you can take right now that will start making a noticeable difference.

In 1994, customer service was the differentiator. In the early 2000s, it became employee engagement. Today, it's all about experience management. By 2030, I don't know what it will be called, but I believe the focus will still be on experiences, the memories we create with individuals. By being tenacious and making experiential changes for employees and customers, you can create systematic and sustainable growth for your organization.

PART I

—

WHY EXPERIENCE MATTERS

If you do a Google search for the term *customer experience*, you will get over a billion results. If you search for *employee experience*, you'll get around 460 million results. Clearly, many people like to talk about these subjects, but somehow, organizations continue to struggle with them.

Read the annual report of any top-twenty company in any market, and you'll see periods in which they talked about transforming their business by focusing on customer experience. You'll also see that these conversations usually go on for two or three years before leaders stop talking about it. Short-term goals often distract leaders from the long-term experience playbook. I sympathize with this struggle. Having spent most of my adult life in the corporate world, I know how tough it can be to juggle the demands of this quarter, half, or year with the long-term strategy of experience.

Rather than trying to make sudden, dramatic company-wide changes, adopt the simple approach of being a little bit better every day.

WHAT'S THE PROBLEM?

In this book, we will explore why experience matters and why it's such a struggle. Through the examples of successful companies, you will see how a relentless focus on delivering better experiences creates sustainable improvements to your business.

Forrester Research released a report in 2017 called "ROI for CX Transformation," based on research into the impact an investment in CX makes on a business.[1] Their conclusion is that in the American market, a one-point improvement in a company's CX index would result in an $873 million increase in revenue for a company in the automotive market, $244 million for a big-box retailer, and $124 million for a traditional bank.

---

1   Dylan Czarnecki and Maxie Schmidt-Subramanian, "The ROI of CX Transformation,"
    Forrester, June 19, 2017, accessed August 13, 2018, https://www.forrester.com/report/
    The+ROI+Of+CX+Transformation/-/E-RES136233

All of this from a one-point improvement in customer experience. What would a 1 percent improvement deliver in your industry?

Think about your organization. Unless you're the leader in your industry, there are no doubt many ways you could improve the experience you deliver to both customers and employees. You are potentially leaving a lot of revenue on the table for your competitors to scoop up.

If you knew for a fact there was more revenue you could potentially capture, how much would the number need to be to get your attention? Ten percent of your current profit? Would $1 million, $5 million, or $100 million be enough? What amount would inspire your team or business to reach the next level? To capture an unfair share of the market opportunity, you just have to move faster than your competitors in delivering a **consistently** better experience.

Improving customer experience will not only prove profitable today, but it can also sustain your business during times of struggle. If you create raving fans, they will be more likely to stick with you if you experience a catastrophic problem in your business, industry, or economy.

The same holds true for employees. Research reveals that the cost of losing an employee is *at least* half their annual wage, due to the expense of recruiting a replacement and training them to become effective in the role.[2] That number is probably understated. Either way, it is money that is better on your bottom line. When you deliver a better experience for your current team, people will want to stick around, which saves you time and money. I also believe that the experience you create for employees has a direct impact on the experience you deliver to customers, so the two are inextricably linked.

Think about the last time you were having a bad day. How hard was it to appear positive to everyone around you? If employees have a negative attitude because of their employment experience that day, week, month, or year, it's going to spill over into the experiences of others.

If you want to allocate resources into one area that will have the broadest and most profound impact on the success of your business at every level, focus on improving experience. Begin by focusing on the experience of your team members. When you create a more fulfilled, satisfied team of committed employees, that will translate into improvements for your customers, and in the end, you will transform your overall business in ways you'd never imagined.

---

2   "The Real Cost of Employee Turnover," *Standard for Success*, accessed August 13, 2018, https://www.standardforsuccess.com/wp-content/uploads/2017/09/Employee_Turnover_Infographic_8.27_2.pdf.

Chapter 1

WHAT IS EXPERIENCE?

One of my strongest memories of my first visit to the United States occurred when I stumbled across a juice store near Grauman's Chinese Theatre in Los Angeles. I didn't even particularly want a fruit smoothie at the time, but I heard the customers chanting and clapping. The line stretched out the door, but everyone appeared to be having a great time. As an outsider, this looked like the place to be. I was amazed that a place selling smoothies could generate such enthusiasm. After all, they were selling a product you can find in almost every mall in America and countries all over the world.

I couldn't resist the hype, so I got in line with everyone else. When I reached the counter, I ordered some juice, paid for it, and put a tip in the tip jar. As soon as my money went into the jar, every employee in the store cheered and shouted, "Thank you!" I was so taken aback that I put another dollar into the tip jar just to experience it again. This time, they all shouted in unison, "Thank you for being a superstar!"

When I got my order, I started to leave, but an employee stopped me.

"No, you have to taste it first," he said. "If you aren't 100 percent happy with it, we will make a new one."

Now, honestly, the drink was only five or six dollars. I figured if it tasted awful, it was no big loss, but I took a sip and said, "It's fine."

The enthusiastic employee smiled and said, "Thanks for being part of our day. We hope to see you again!"

During that first trip, I spent five days in Los Angeles, and I was so impressed with the experience that I went back to the juice store every day. The product was decent, not amazing. It quenched my thirst, which was all I needed. However, the atmosphere and experience created such a strong memory that I can still recall it vividly fifteen years later. The fruit juice could have come straight out of a bottle, and the experience would still have made it feel worthwhile.

With their attention to delivering an amazing experience,

they achieved two things. First, they successfully delivered the product I wanted and made it feel effortless. Even waiting in the queue didn't take too long. In fact, the enthusiasm made it fun to wait my turn. Second, they created a connection with me and every other customer. Not only did they interact with me in an exciting, fun way, but I also got to see them interact with other customers. It was the customer interaction that drew me into the store in the first place.

CREATING LIFELONG MEMORIES

Powerful customer experiences like this create connections that turn into lifelong memories. Nobody remembers a typical visit to the grocery store down the street, but they will remember a fun or exciting interaction with store employees. Consider your own business. Could you deliver an experience so amazing that your customers will think about it for years to come? The juice shop in Los Angeles didn't have a particularly special product, but I'll never forget the experience I had there. Anytime I'm in Los Angeles, I will try to go back.

When I first visited, I saw ten employees working in the juice shop that day. Chances are at least one of them was having a bad day. Maybe one of them had had a fight with their spouse that morning or had gotten a flat tire on the way to work. Maybe one of them was worried about paying the rent that week. If so, it didn't show. In the moment, they were completely focused on creating the customer experience. They left their worries at the door and had fun interacting with customers in a genuine way.

An amazing experience inspires customers to speak about your business, but an ordinary and forgettable experience usually leads to customer silence. The feeling you create produces the result.

WHAT ARE YOU OVERLOOKING?

When you work as an experience professional, you tend to become laser-focused and highly analytical about the experiences you have. You learn to become critical of even the smallest things, and when you have a great time at a hotel or restaurant or during an Uber ride, you tend to break down the why.

Conversely, minor annoyances, such as the dust on the counter that most people don't notice or the Uber driver who won't get out and help you with your bags, stand out. Apply this same critical lens to the experience you deliver to your customers, and you will begin to identify shortcomings and areas of needed improvement.

As part of her new job, a colleague of mine inherited contact center operations at a large organization, and she emailed me to ask my thoughts on implementing improvements. I was happy to help. The first thing I did was pick up the phone and pretend to be a customer at the contact center. I called three or four times, so when I spoke to my friend and former colleague, I could speak from experience about needed improvements. By identifying the low-hanging fruit, I was able to recommend some efficient, easy improvements for quick wins.

I visited a furniture store recently in which everything initially seemed just fine. The visual merchandising team had done a great job of creating the displays. However, it was a multilevel store, and as I ascended the escalator, I got a good look at the backside of the displays. What I saw I can only describe as *years of accumulated filth*. Dirt and dust had built up like snow, and my immediate thought was, "How hard would it be to dust back there once a month?"

My next thought was, "If they can't bother to clean up behind the display cases, what else are they failing to do behind the scenes?" As leaders, these are the kinds of things you must be aware of. You are responsible for the experience you deliver to customers. I'm not suggesting you get bogged down in the negative. Rather, a good leader focuses on finding opportunities to improve in a positive way.

Here, I have shared with you two simple examples of how

walking in the shoes of your customers or employees can inform your focus areas. Do you regularly ask yourself, "What is the experience of my team members today? What is the experience of my customers today?"

When was the last time you did a mystery shop of your own teams? Often, the answers you're looking for are in the experiences you haven't yet personally undertaken. For that reason, the first step to improving your customer or team experience is to walk a mile, or even just a few inches, in the shoes of customers and team members.

In regard to your team, the experience a new employee has during their first few days on the job has the biggest impact on whether or not they stay with you long term. Think back on your first days at the best and worst companies you ever worked for. The lingering memories you have define what I mean by experience. Positive or negative, they left a mark in your memory that influence your expectations to this day.

Now, more than ever, you need to consider the feelings you inspire and the memories you create in everything you do.

CREATING STRONG ADVOCATES OR FIERCE DETRACTORS

Both employees and customers can become strong

advocates or fierce detractors of your company, which is why we are focusing on both throughout this book. An employee can make the job of attracting and retaining talent easier by speaking well of your company to friends and family.

They advocate for your business in the way they treat people even when they're not on the job. When someone at the dinner table says they're having a problem with your company's product or service, the way that employee responds, even though they aren't technically at work, can foster brand loyalty. Employee advocates play a huge role in the sustainability of your business, growing your customer base, increasing revenue, and saving you money, which is why the experience you create for them is of such vital importance.

We're also focusing on customers because they are, after all, the consumers of the experience you create. Fifteen years from now, they might not remember the refrigerator they bought from you, but they will remember the experience they had while buying it. What sort of memory is created for a customer when they buy an appliance, then hear that the store can deliver it only on Friday between noon and six o'clock? That forces them to take time off work, interrupting their lives just so they can have the privilege of receiving the appliance they paid for. That's not a pleasant memory.

We're not limiting our discussion to appliance stores, of course. This book is built for any business, and the tips, hints, and valuable insights on building brand advocates from both customers and employees are designed to be transferable.

Personally, I've worked in seven different industries, and I've seen the importance of experience in all of them, particularly as it relates to three things: success, effort, and human connection. We will address all three of these in greater detail later on.

We will also address the key points in creating consistency of experience, whether in a single, multisite, or franchise operation. When someone interacts with your brand, whether it happens online or in a traditional brick-and-mortar store, consistency is essential. The last experience someone has becomes the new norm, especially if it's a peak experience. It becomes what they expect every time, so you must improve the experience in a sustainable way.

I believe anyone can improve customer experience overnight, but a better way to approach customer experience is to embed an experience mindset in the hearts and minds of your teams. Doing this takes time and commitment, but it rewards you with sustainable growth and results.

Here's the key: customer experience *begins* with employee

experience. Between the two, if you can focus on improving only one, focus on your employees, because more engaged and excited employees will directly improve the experience for customers.

A RELENTLESS OBSESSION

As I mentioned in the introduction, I created a successful computer sales company in 1994, but what differentiated my business wasn't the processing power of the computers I sold or the price I offered. Instead, it was the level of customer service I delivered. By the mid-2000s, employee engagement had become a hot topic in major organizations in many industries. Today, most companies offer some kind of engagement survey every year.

Despite this increased focus, companies that can effectively focus on both employee and customer experience in a consistent way remain in the minority. The ability to create those positive experiences day after day, week after week, year after year with tenacity continues to evade many leaders, so if you develop a relentless obsession about improving experience, you will stand apart.

Throughout this book, I will provide effective ways to create positive experiences that become the stories people share about your business. It's in those stories that you connect to new customers and new employees, driving your business forward.

Chapter 2

WILL IT GO AWAY?

In 1998, at the age of nineteen, I joined the wholesale business of an Australian company called Telstra, which was Australia's largest telecommunications company at the time, providing a range of telecommunication services for homes, small businesses, and corporate and government customers.

I began in the wholesale division, and while I appreciated everything I learned in that role, I eventually stopped feeling valued by the company. I left to become a founding team member for a brand-new contact center in a chartered accounting firm. As the second hire, my job was to help establish a team that could deliver salary-packaging support to the state of Queensland's government employees.

I had never been in an accounting firm, had no professional accounting training, and had to learn relevant skills quickly. While I thrived on the challenge, the job was limited in its growth potential. I couldn't go far on the corporate ladder, and to be fair, my heart was still at Telstra. At Telstra, I'd felt like I was part of something bigger, and I missed it. When I got an opportunity to rejoin Telstra in a newly created department called the Center for Customer Experience, I jumped at it. It proved to be one of my favorite professional experiences.

Despite the name, the Center for Customer Experience didn't focus on strategizing or improving customer experience. Instead, our purpose was to manage existing customers when they experienced a delay in receiving services. In some cases, the customers we dealt with had waited months to get their new phone services connected, and as you can imagine, they often had strong feelings about the delay—*frustration* is a polite way of putting it.

The company had identified these delays as a pain point in the organization. With new competition starting in the Australian telecommunications market, customers gained access to alternatives, so Telstra knew they had to do something to address the problem. During my time there, I created and implemented customer-service training programs that went above and beyond the norm, surpassing customer expectations with the hope of mitigating frustrations.

Since then, Telstra has developed an entire department focused on transformative customer experiences, covering all aspects of the company. Like many companies, they have realized the growing relevance of customer experience.

BETTER THAN LOW PRICES

Forrester Research and Capgemini SE have both done excellent research on company differentiation, concluding that organizations that don't (or can't) compete on price must differentiate through experience.[3] Many companies reach an absolute floor in their product prices. They simply can't afford to go any lower if they want to remain profitable, but they still have to compete somehow.

It has been my long-held belief that a race to the lowest price is the wrong strategy. A race to the top in delivering segment-leading experiences is the winning long-term strategy.

When competitors arose, Telstra wouldn't (or couldn't) offer the cheapest phone services, so they focused on pairing the best product with an unrelenting commitment to improving the customer experience. Today, they talk

---

3   Laura Ramos, "Back2Basics: Why B2B Marketers Should Differentiate on Customer Experience," *Forrester*, May 16, 2018, accessed August 13, 2018, https://go.forrester.com/blogs/b2b-marketers-should-differentiate-on-customer-experiences/.

about customer experience in everything they do. As they say on their website, "We believe the more connected people are, the more opportunities they have. That's why we help create a brilliant connected future for everyone, [every day]."[4] According to the company website, their strategy, called Telstra2022, includes delivering market-leading customer experiences.[5]

As the company evolved over the years, the focus changed periodically, sometimes with negative results. For a while, they had a relentless focus on engineering excellence. After privatization, they went through a period of focusing on cost reduction at the expense of customer service. As someone who worked at Telstra during the privatization period, I can personally attest to the many "barbecue conversations" among team members about the negative impact this had across the company.

It was the work of CEO David Thodey, who joined the company in 2001, that turned things around. I had the pleasure of working in his division when he was the group managing director of Telstra Enterprise and Government. During that time, I gained insight into David's vision, and his focus was on the experience of customers and employees.

---

4   Simon K., "Proud Past, Brilliant Future," Telstra, accessed August 13, 2018, https://www.telstra.com.au/aboutus/our-company.

5   "Our Corporate Strategy," Telstra, accessed August 13, 2018, https://www.telstra.com.au/aboutus/our-company/future/Ourcorporatestrategy.

David Thodey was appointed CEO of Telstra in 2009. I wasn't with the company at the time, but the media, and my friends, regularly reported on the ways he was igniting a passion for delivering an experience that emphasized the lifetime value proposition of customers. This shift dramatically reduced the number of incoming complaints and created many loyal brand advocates.

Complaints are time-consuming, costly to manage, and they diminish advocacy and loyalty, which is why they are a key factor companies can use to measure performance. This is another reason why customer experience will never cease to matter. Even if we're calling it something else in ten to fifteen years, the fundamental need to connect with customers will remain.

FOCUS ON THE BOTTOM LINE

Some managers think experience is the "fluffy stuff," because chief customer experience officers don't always take a commercial view of the work they do. Historically, the focus has been on creating individual touchpoints with customers, such as greetings. While these kinds of moments are important, they fail to view experience as a primary factor in helping a business grow and remain profitable.

As CX and EX professionals (or, as I like to call it, XM:

eXperience Management), we must begin to link our work to the commercial outcome of our organizations. When you do that, you not only reinforce the work you do, but you also ensure you have a legitimate seat at the executive table by contributing to a long-term business result that makes shareholders happy. Customer and employee experience provides a massive return on investment if done in a sustainable way that grows repeat and referral business.

Of course, everything you do in customer experience doesn't have to create an immediate commercial impact, but you have to be able to demonstrate ROI. When you can show that customer experience delivers a positive impact to the brand and balance sheet, you will be able to ask for more investment.

When executives understand the ROI you deliver, they will be more willing to provide the resources you need to accelerate your programs even further. I would love to give every new recruit in my organization free lunch for a month or the latest shiny object that we sell, but the return wouldn't necessarily justify the investment. Having said that, of course, providing ways for new recruits to connect with the brand, its heritage, its future, and its products is important. Later in this book, we will explore how a company can do this—and yes, sometimes it includes a free lunch.

Another trap XM professionals fall into is believing their own press, convinced that their program is always right. We must always look critically at our programs and tweak them so they continue to deliver results. Doing this constantly reinforces the notion that what we do contributes to the bottom line.

Then again, even some of the softer skills of customer experience, such as the way you greet people or manage communication, are important and difficult to deliver sustainably. Like everything else, improvements must be rolled out in a commercially sensible way.

UNUSUAL AND OUTRAGEOUS IDEAS

As products and services become more global, organizations are becoming more similar, making it increasingly important to create a differentiated experience for employees and customers. Some companies are trying concepts and ideas that previous generations would have considered unusual or even outrageous. For example, it is widely reported that Google provides employees with the freedom to spend up to 20 percent of their working time on so-called side projects. These side projects don't need leadership approval and can be big or small. Some of them have led to products we now use every day, most notably Gmail. That's the kind of differentiation that makes them stand out as an employer.

Many companies are doing great work in humanizing the customer experience during times of devastation, such as financial companies forgiving loan payments when a loved one has passed away or phone companies providing free mobile services during a natural disaster. These organizations understand that the experience they deliver will create long-lasting memories that will sustain them in a way they can feel proud of.

Consider Zappos, the well-known American shoe and apparel retailer. They've become famous around the world for their customer experience. In fact, if you do a Google search for "Zappos's customer experience," you will get more than 2.7 million responses, the vast majority from customers gushing about their interactions with the company. The CEO of Zappos, Tony Hsieh, has talked at length about their success, which he attributes largely to the culture they've created in the organization.

During an interview with Micah Solomon at *Forbes*, Hsieh emphasized the effort they've made to create and sustain a culture obsessed with customers.[6] Famously, they pay employees to leave the company if they aren't fully on board with the culture. That speaks to the power of the

---

6   Micah Solomon, "Is the Proudly-Weird Culture of Tony Hsieh's Zappos Also Its Customer Service Secret?" *Forbes*, June 19, 2017, accessed August 13, 2018, https://www.forbes.com/sites/micahsolomon/2017/06/19/is-the-proudly-weird-culture-of-tony-hsiehs-zappos-its-customer-service-success-secret.

organization, and they have enjoyed years of significant growth, resulting in their acquisition by Amazon.

As a testimony to the strength of their culture, they've managed to keep it intact even after becoming part of a larger organization. In fact, even though I live in Australia, I wait until my trips to the United States to buy shoes from Zappos because I know I can trust the experience. They have earned my loyalty in everything they do. The consistency of the experience they deliver means that even in countries such as Australia, where they don't operate, they are still routinely referred to at customer experience conferences as a case study.

I visited Zappos for the first time in 2008, but I'd already spoken to them beforehand through their Twitter account. On Twitter, they gave me hotel recommendations. Can you imagine? A shoe company giving me hotel recommendations on social media! While I was writing this book, I decided to test them again, so I tweeted at them, told them I would be staying at the Ritz-Carlton in Marina del Rey, and mentioned that I needed a haircut. True to form, Zappos's Twitter account gave me three recommendations for places to get a good haircut. Of course, they aren't experts in the haircut industry, and they probably used Yelp to find their recommendations. Still, they demonstrated their focus on creating and maintaining an ongoing connection with me. This approach speaks to how deeply ingrained their customer-oriented culture is in every part of their organization.

In 2018, I was urgently in need of a particular style and color of Nike shoe for an upcoming event. I sent the company a tweet, and they replied that they didn't carry that particular item. However, they told me they had located what I was looking for at another store, a competitor, and they offered me directions.

They understood that a friendly gesture, even if it sent me to a competitor, would contribute to my sense of loyalty and advocacy. After all, here I am praising Zappos rather than the competitor I ultimately bought that pair of shoes from.

Can your company, can your team, can *you* become this obsessed in helping customers achieve success?

Which-50, an Australian news service, interviewed me recently and asked, "When it comes to customer experience, whose responsibility is it?" The answer is clear. It's the responsibility of every single person at the organization to ensure that the experience they deliver both internally and externally consistently aligns with the culture. Every interaction with a customer at every level matters.

Ten to fifteen years ago, organizations were furiously

debating about the necessity of customer service. Some wanted to sideline it because they saw customer service as a cost center rather than a change agent in the business. Since then, there's been a significant push to make customer service, and the long-lasting memories an experience creates, at the forefront—a trail blazed by pioneers such as Jeanne Bliss, who in many respects created the chief customer officer (CCO) role.

For a CCO, customer experience ensures that the company grows through repeat and referral business. After all, word of mouth is the cheapest and loudest form of marketing.

THINKING LONG TERM

United Airlines provides a clear example of what happens when an organization fails to maintain a long-term focus on customer experience. In 2017, the airline gained international attention when a customer was aggressively removed from a seat he had legally purchased. Video footage of airport security dragging him off the plane went viral and led to widespread condemnation.

In May 2017, the CEO publicly vowed that United Airlines would become more customer-focused, but in 2018, the airline hit the news again when a family pet died in transit, allegedly as a result of its handling by the company.

This goes to show how challenging it can be to transform customer experience. As I said, it takes a commitment at every level of an organization.

I'm not suggesting that companies have to maintain a perfect track record. Every organization is run by people, and people are bound to make mistakes from time to time. However, two very public, very negative customer interactions in two years is cause for alarm, especially because the CEO had already publicly committed to focusing more on customers.

This is what happens when you don't invest enough in experience starting at the senior level. By the time the neglect becomes apparent, the damage is done, and it can't be fixed overnight. In the case of United Airlines, it created the appearance that a promise was made and broken, which is calamitous for customer loyalty. Of course, I believe that any company has the ability to transform over time and become famous for the (positive) experiences they deliver.

On the opposite end of the spectrum, we have the example of Southwest Airlines, a company that has been relentless in delivering a phenomenal customer experience from day one. Southwest was established in 1967, and they are the only long-term airline in the continental United States to make a profit every single year, even though they are a value-based airline. They've accomplished this feat by focusing on, first, delivering an excellent experience for their employees and, second, translating that into a high-quality consistent for customers.

WEATHERING MISSTEPS

It's important to remember that being obsessed with customer and employee experience isn't about always getting it right. There is great value in learning from failures. When a company is truly obsessed with customer and employee experience, they build a reputation that allows them to weather the occasional misstep. Southwest has had their own missteps and public criticism. There is even a Twitter account, @Southwest_sux, where people regularly share their frustrations about the airline. In an example of a misstep, *Inc.com* reports that Southwest Airlines landed at the wrong airport, seven miles away from its intended destination.[7] As a result, they are being sued for $74,999. Despite this misstep and others, the brand has established itself as a leader in customer experience among low-cost carriers.

In 2018, they were rated highest in customer satisfaction in the J.D. Power 2018 North America Airline Satisfaction

---

7   Bill Murphy Jr., "A Passenger Sued Southwest Airlines for Exactly $74,999, and It's Totally Brilliant. Here's Why," Inc., March 11, 2018, accessed August 13, 2018, https://www.inc.com/bill-murphy-jr/a-passenger-sued-southwest-airlines-for-exactly-74999-its-totally-brilliant-heres-why.html.

Study.[8] In the same year, they also won the TripAdvisor Traveler's Choice Award for airlines.[9] The company's enduring focus on customer and employee experience allows them to continue to grow and, importantly, overcome their missteps.

Southwest might not be the airline for everyone, but it doesn't have to be. All they have to do is keep the promises they make to customers and employees by maintaining a crystal-clear focus on the experience, constantly communicating it throughout the organization.

INVESTING IN THE COMMUNITY

For an Australian example, we can look to the home improvement store Bunnings Warehouse, which is by far the biggest hardware store in the nation, similar to Home Depot in the United States. Bunnings has had a number of competitors, including Masters, a joint venture of Woolworths and Lowe's. Masters was founded in 2011 but closed its doors in 2016. Although a number

---

8   Southwest Airlines Newsroom, "Southwest Airlines Ranks Highest in Customer Satisfaction among Low-Cost Carriers in North America According to J.D. Power," June 15, 2018, accessed August 14, 2018, https://www.swamedia.com/releases/release-63dd6d3a3fb0751687938f48891d7a4f-southwest-airlines-ranks-highest-in-customer-satisfaction-among-low-cost-carriers-in-north-america-according-to-jd-power.

9   Southwest Airlines Newsroom, "Southwest Airlines Wins 2018 TripAdvisor Traveler's Choice Awards for Airlines," April 9, 2018, accessed August 14, 2018, https://www.swamedia.com/releases/release-de080387b716f7f68a21d1f8644c871a-southwest-airlines-wins-2018-tripadvisor-travelers-choice-awards-for-airlines.

of factors contributed to the failure of Masters, one of the clear differentiators at Bunnings was the customer experience. Team members at Bunnings are easily recognizable, and a customer can always approach them to ask for help. Team members will either point the way or lead the customer directly to the item they need. On the other hand, Masters has more of a self-service model. In my numerous trips to the store, I never once saw a team member leading a customer to an item. While the self-service model might seem appealing, it also makes customers feel less appreciated.

Bunnings invested in a better customer experience, an experience based on consistency and ease. At the same time, taking a page out of Ace Hardware's playbook, they embedded themselves in the community, serving in various ways in the cities where they are located. It's not just about the friendly greeting you give when customers walk through the door. It's also about the ways you interact with the community around your business. It's about becoming more than merely a retailer.

Every Bunnings across the nation offers space for charity groups to have barbecue fund-raisers, where they can cook the typical sausages and onions while raising money for their cause. In fact, it has become an Australian tradition to go to Bunnings for a sausage to support the charity of the week. They have created a powerful touchpoint with Australian communities that strengthens the brand, doing far more to create customer loyalty than competitive pricing alone could ever achieve.

Of course, Bunnings is not without its competition. They still have to contend with companies such as Home Timber & Hardware and Mitre 10. While Bunnings is arguably the most recognizable home improvement retail brand in Australia, they don't rest on their laurels. They remain passionate about their customers.

Customer satisfaction benchmarking completed by Roy Morgan in 2017 showed that Bunnings is number one in customer satisfaction, with a score of 89 percent, an increase of 0.1 percent from the previous year.[10]

Even though 0.1 percent might not seem like much, it shouldn't be scoffed at. Most companies would love to have a customer satisfaction score of 80 percent or more, but Bunnings clearly continued to tweak and improve their approach. At the same time, Home Timber & Hardware dropped 0.4 percent.

The home improvement market is a tough one that requires consistent elevating focus, and Bunnings has

---

10   Roy Morgan, "Bunnings 'Sizzling' with High Customer Satisfaction," October 27, 2017, accessed August 14, 2018, http://www.roymorgan.com/findings/7393-csa-results-september-2017-hardware-stores-201710270308.

become the market leader not simply because of their products but also because people trust them to provide a good experience with every interaction.

A MANAGER'S RESPONSIBILITY

One of a manager's responsibilities is to help team members improve their job performance. We've all dealt with employees who are content with the status quo. "I just want to do my job, leave on time, and go home. I don't want any added stress." However, if team members don't improve, then they won't be able to keep up with the job as it evolves, whether due to technological advances, customer expectations, or the organization's demands.

A manager is successful when they have a highly engaged, efficient, and successful team, but it's difficult to do that if you have high turnover. That's why I say your first responsibility is to create and deliver experiences for your employees. When you do that, you make people want to stay, and when an employee develops loyalty to the company, your investment in them delivers a much higher ROI. Instead of using your money to constantly train new employees, you're paying to enhance the skills and efficiencies of existing team members.

Once you've created an engaging experience for employees, you should work with your team to differentiate the customer experience. Failing to do so in today's more competitive market is dangerous to the future of your company.

"A Kodak moment" is a catchphrase known for generations, a relic of a time when Kodak was the market leader in photographic film. Anything worth photographing was a Kodak moment. However, in 2012, the company filed for Chapter 11 bankruptcy protection.

Kodak wasn't simply a victim of the tech boom. In 2016, *Harvard Business Review* reported that in 1975, a highly engaged engineer at Kodak named Steve Sasson developed the first prototype for a digital camera.[11] According to Sasson, his management team said, "The innovation is cute, but don't tell anyone about it."

Kodak had clearly created an environment where people were committed to the organization and developing groundbreaking products. However, the company failed to find ways to harness that potential, which led to massive negative disruption to the business.

---

11   Scott Anthony, "Kodak's Downfall Wasn't about Technology," *Harvard Business Review*, July 15, 2016, accessed August 14, 2018, https://hbr.org/2016/07/kodaks-downfall-wasnt-about-technology.

DISRUPT YOURSELF

Customer experience, sales, service, and business thought leader Scott McKain,[12] on his *Project Distinct* podcast, reminds us about another company that has suffered as a result of disruption: Gillette. The pioneers in disposable razors, Gillette enjoyed market leader advantage for many years. However, their focus drifted away from the customer, which paved the way for a surge of disrupters such as Dollar Shave Club.

Although they are the founders of the disposable razor, Gillette has been losing market share in the very product they invented because they've made it difficult for customers to obtain the product. When you walk into a supermarket, Gillette razors are often locked in a display case so they won't be stolen.

These disruptors looked at the **friction points** of the typical retail disposable-razor product and removed as many negative interactions as possible. To buy a humble disposable Gillette razor, you often have to find someone with a key to the cabinet they are stored in, or battle a safety mechanism to remove it from the shelf.

Compare that to Dollar Shave Club, which has not only made their razors affordable but also ships the product right to the customer's door every month at the same

12   https://scottmckain.com/

time. Whether or not the product is superior to the Gillette product, they've delivered an experience that is a huge differentiator, making ease of access their primary concern.

If you identify friction points with your products or services faster than your competitors, you can act quickly to disrupt yourself before anyone else gets the chance. Doing this safeguards your business against disruptors.

Think about your own company. Is there a different angle you can take on the experience of acquiring your product? The subscription model of Dollar Shave Club might not be right for you, but is there another way you could make it easier for customers to get it?

The taxi industry provides another example of what happens when nothing is done to address friction points in the customer experience. As a result, Uber, Didi Chuxing, and Lyft have created a completely different experience by embracing the sharing economy. Like taxis, they still get people from point A to point B, but they use mobile devices to make it easier and more convenient. The opportunity existed because the taxi industry, despite having plenty of drivers who were great at their jobs, stopped focusing on the customer experience.

Uber, Didi Chuxing, and Lyft also improved the payment

process. No longer did customers have to pull out cash or a credit card, because payment is handled entirely through apps. Not only is this more convenient for customers, but it's also safer for drivers, who no longer have to carry cash in their vehicles to make change.

Friction is the enemy of positive word of mouth. If you fail to take advantage of opportunities to eliminate friction points, there's a good chance a competitor will. Consider how the news and newspapers have been disrupted by social media. Consider how major airlines have been disrupted by JetBlue and Southwest.

Take a step back and look at your own company and industry. Find ways to deliver from a different angle; consider ways to remove friction points. If you can do that, you will stand out from the pack. Customers will notice and begin to tell your story.

Chapter 3

———

EXPERIENCE DRIVES BUSINESS RESULTS

After five years at Telstra, I had the opportunity to move to Australia's second largest telecommunications company, Optus, one of the first Telstra competitors to arise as a result of government deregulation. For many years in Australia, customers who were underwhelmed by their experiences at Telstra had no other options, so the opportunity for disruption was huge when Optus hit the market. Much like the taxi industry, Telstra hadn't been laser-focused on customer experience because they didn't have to confront their friction points.

Optus entered the market with the simple slogan "Yes, Optus." The implication wasn't that customers should say no to Telstra, but that Optus would say yes to customers more than their competitors. To accomplish this, they galvanized their organization from within around the concept of experience. When they brought on a new team member, they always asked them, "How do we say yes to customers?" It was woven into the DNA of the organization.

This focus helped Optus experience tremendous growth, but with their expansion into new fields, they encountered new challenges. I started as a customer service manager in the B2B space, and I had a portfolio of customers that included iconic brands such as General Motors (Holden in Australia), Nestlé, and various government organizations. My team was responsible for providing and managing end to end the full suite of telecommunication products: everything from mobile phones and fixed lines to complex data networks. Ultimately, we were responsible for delivering bespoke solutions to around thirty large corporate customers representing hundreds of millions in revenue.

In the beginning, we had numerous unhappy customers who were dissatisfied with the level of service they'd been receiving. We were given a mandate to turn things around, so one of my first decisions as manager was to rally my team around the brand. The "Yes, Optus" slogan had power to it, so I reintroduced it to the team.

"How do we get a yes from the customer?" I asked. "What

improvements can we make to the experience that will generate such a response?"

A yes from a customer didn't primarily mean a sale. Instead, it referred to an exclamation of excitement from being wowed by an experience.

By focusing on experience, we gained some quick wins, retaining tens of millions of dollars that were at risk, increasing customer satisfaction by 24 percent in the first three months, and increasing staff retention by 30 percent. We reduced the cost to serve by delivering more for the same cost, and we delivered more sales because customers came to trust that we would deliver—a trust that hadn't always existed before.

WHAT'S YOUR GUIDING NORTH STAR?

We delivered to our team by making it clear what we wanted and expected from them, creating a guiding North Star, and we celebrated every success. By helping customers achieve success with as little effort as possible, while also bolstering and guiding our team, we turned things around and helped put Optus on the right track.

For our call center team, we had three main goals: to meet customer key performance indicators (KPIs), to celebrate successes with them, and to help them develop and learn new skills. We also analyzed every success to see how much effort was required so we could find ways to minimize the effort.

Once our team was consistently hitting their main goals, our next step was to teach them to create relationships at every level. That meant creating relationships between call center associates and the companies buying from us. If something went wrong, we wanted our customers to trust that we would take care of it because of the strong connection they had with our associates. We wanted to feel connected to the senior decision makers in the companies we served so we would always know what their concerns were and where to focus our attention.

It isn't rocket science, but we learned that the key to winning at both customer and employee experience is a relentless and consistent pursuit of improvement. We'll look at that in more depth in a later chapter, unpacking specific principles for improving experience. As part of that effort, we made sure our team members had knowledge about our customers. In order to deliver a personalized experience, you have to know your customers so you can apply that knowledge. This has been true in every industry I've worked in.

We also made sure our team knew how to navigate all of the processes and systems we'd put in place. If you don't do that, it becomes difficult for your team to deliver a good experience. People tend to either love or hate processes; there's rarely a middle ground. However, processes are a fantastic way of delivering consistency. While they don't guarantee a memorable experience, they allow transactions to be completed more easily so team members can focus on building a human connection with the person they're serving. When processes are in place, managers can also focus on creating human connections with their team members, and it's these human connections that produce long-lasting memories.

By setting a North Star to guide our team, creating knowledge around processes and systems, and providing training so they could get beyond mere transactions to make real connections, we grew revenue, reduced turnover, and enabled our team to meet metrics—such as average call time—that hadn't been met in years.

When I first got there, many customers were on the verge of leaving the organization, but our focus on delivering consistent experiences profoundly increased retention and grew customer accounts. This led to numerous team members advancing their careers, which goes to show that when you improve customer experience, you open up opportunities for yourself and your team.

PREMIUM PRICES FOR EXPERIENCE

Ten years after the introduction of the iPhone, customers still line up outside of stores for the launch of the newest version. People aren't simply chasing a shiny new object. Apple has relentlessly pursued the delivery of an experience that people will pay a premium price for, even if the iPhone (arguably) doesn't have all of the features of its competitors. It's the experience that creates brand loyalty.

I should know. I've been a loyal iPhone owner for many years. Why do I keep coming back? On more than one occasion, I've dropped my phone and shattered the screen or dropped it in water, and every time, the process for getting it repaired or replaced has been seamless. Apple has always made it super-easy to resolve the problem, exceeding my expectations. There has also been the occasional "surprise and delight" moment to reinforce the company's appreciation of my loyalty.

Even though the iPhone isn't the cheapest on the market, they've built lifetime fans who are prepared to pay extra because they trust the experience. They have elevated the brand through word-of-mouth advocacy, including what I've written about them in this book.

When I worked for Target, we launched a limited edition collaboration with the famous designer Missoni, and

Target's retail website crashed from the number of customers trying to purchase the products online. It took the organization almost twenty-four hours to get the website back up and running. Because Target is focused on customer experience, we pivoted and designated a large part of our contact center, which normally fields complaints and general enquiries, to sell the products by phone.

We declared, "All hands on deck," and called in our off-shift contact center workers to field orders. As a result, we lost very little revenue while the website was down. We grossed more than $1 million in sales through the contact center, helped others arrange in-store pickup, and ultimately ensured sales were completed that otherwise would have been lost.

Most traditional businesses view contact centers as an expense, but we proved they can be transformed into experience centers that help customers achieve what they want. In this particular instance, we added profit to the business with very little additional cost.

IT'S NOT TOO LATE TO CHANGE

Based on comments he's made to the media in the past, Ryanair's CEO Michael O'Leary hasn't always loved customers. However, in 2014, *The Guardian* declared,

"Ryanair puts 32% jump in profits down to being nicer."[13] The same article quotes O'Leary as saying, "If I had known being nicer to customers was going to work so well, I would have started many years ago."

In 2018, *Fortune* magazine reported, in their annual "100 Best Companies to Work For," that the great companies on the list have lower turnover, achieve higher levels of customer satisfaction, and have a stronger financial performance.[14] In fact, they perform, on average, 5 percent better than their competitors. Wouldn't we all love a 5 percent bump in performance?

Whether you're a small business or a multinational corporation, paying attention to customer and employee experience will have a remarkable impact on your organization's success and sustainability at every level. In the next chapter, we'll examine how you can measure experience. I'll show you the best places to focus on your experience transformation so you can further build your brand and boost customer loyalty. We'll also further explore ways to drive transformation that will lead to your personal success as well as the success of your team and organization.

---

13   Gwyn Topham, "Ryanair Puts 32% Jump in Profits Down to Being Nicer," *The Guardian*, November 3, 2014, accessed August 14, 2018, https://www.theguardian.com/business/2014/nov/03/ryanair-raises-profit-surge-winter-bookings.

14   "100 Best Companies to Work For," *Fortune*, accessed August 14, 2018, http://fortune.com/best-companies/.

PART II

HOW INDIVIDUALS AND ORGANIZATIONS MEASURE EXPERIENCE

We're all human, and ultimately, the lenses employees use to measure experience aren't all that different from the lenses customers use. In this next section, we will explore the ways people measure an experience with an organization and how it is influenced by their interactions so you can drive improvements for both customers and employees.

As a specific tool, we will discuss touchpoint surveys and how you can leverage the insights garnered from them. Along the way, we will begin to hone your ability to judge experiences, creating a yardstick by which you can measure the success of your organization and a pathway to get where you want to go.

Chapter 4

SUCCESS, EASE, AND CONNECTION FOR THE CUSTOMER

Generally speaking, customers and employees measure their experiences through three lenses: success, ease or effort, and the human or emotional connection. Success, the most basic of the three, means customers are able to achieve what they set out to achieve, whether buying a soda at the local 7-Eleven or buying a new house.

Customers expect to expend some effort achieving whatever their version of success is. Ideally, a company enables customers to achieve success with less effort than they expect. Doing this contributes to loyalty and advocacy, helping to grow your business in a sustainable way.

In general, a human connection means treating customers with dignity and respect. Sometimes this can be as simple as using their name when speaking to them. Other times, it comes from showing genuine care for their wellbeing. In all cases, it's about removing bureaucracy from the interaction and dealing with a customer at a human level. Empower your team to have the freedom to create connections with customers so they can embed the brand into the community. Invest the time and skills to teach your team members how to create these moments of authentic connection in every interaction with customers.

TRANSCEND THE OBVIOUS

Achieving success is the most basic requirement of a positive customer experience. If you've ever bought a home, consider the last conversation you had with a mortgage broker. From the outset, you measured success as getting a home loan approved, but is that all you were looking for?

You see, success is measured by both expressed and unexpressed desires. It's important to dig deeper to understand the full measure of what customers hope to achieve. In the case of your home loan, maybe you also measured success as getting a bigger home so you could start a family. Maybe some life circumstance or change motivated your desire to acquire a home. Whatever the case, it's important for your mortgage broker to know these things so they can create an experience you will never forget.

Recently, while giving a presentation to a large bank in Australia, I told them that we need to transcend the obvious. A mortgage is merely a starting point for what customers are trying to achieve. I encouraged them to look beyond the mortgage to what the customer is actually trying to achieve, whether that's creating equity in real estate, acquiring stable housing for a growing family, or something else. If you focus on only the mortgage (or whatever your expressed product is), you miss the opportunity to connect with the customer and celebrate their real success.

The stated need isn't always the best way to celebrate with a customer. A mortgage is debt, and people don't like debt. You're not necessarily going to celebrate a $500,000 loan, but you can celebrate that the customer bought a nice home with plenty of room for their growing family and a big yard their children can play in.

Of course, every situation is not as clear-cut as buying a house. When I worked in telecommunications, I once had the executive assistant of a senior customer call us, frantic because her boss had lost his mobile phone. He was flying out of town that very day, and she needed a replacement right away. The company could have followed the standard process and shipped a new phone to his destination. Instead, the customer service associate arranged to have a colleague meet the customer at the airport and deliver the new phone in person.

This was an excellent example of a B2B transaction that extended beyond the immediate request. It made both the company and the customer's executive assistant look successful in the eyes of the boss.

MAKE IT AS EASY AS POSSIBLE

Amazon is famous for its one-click purchase option. They patented the design, and as I understand it, a number of organizations have licensed the technology. For Amazon, the underlying benefit is that customers can achieve success very easily. If you find a great book you want, you don't have to search for your credit card or confirm shipping details. A single click completes the purchase.

This is Amazon's impressive answer to the question, "How can we deliver a better experience for our customer?" It's a question you need to ask yourself. Consider the story of Great Britain's Olympic rowing team. When they failed to make the rowing finals in 1998, they became laser-focused on answering the question, "What will make the boat go faster?" Any idea or activity that didn't help answer that question got sidelined. This made preparing for the next Olympics easier because they weren't wasting effort on tasks that didn't directly improve their speed. What single question would get your team laser-focused on improving customer or employee experience?

Recently, I was considering the process supermarkets use at their self-checkout lanes. During purchase, they first provide some kind of "pay now" button and then make you choose cash, credit, or debit. That seems like one unnecessary step. Why not eliminate the first option and simply ask customers to select their transaction type? Anytime you can find ways to eliminate extra steps for a customer, you make it easier for them to achieve success.

In the early 2000s, I booked an anniversary vacation with my partner. The memory of it is still loud and clear in my mind but not for the reasons you might think. As you can imagine, this had a lot of emotional significance for us, so I wanted to make sure everything was perfect. Unfortunately, the hotel sent me the wrong directions. Because of roadwork in the area, the directions led us away from the hotel. When we finally found our way to the hotel, they put us in the wrong room type at check-in. They corrected the booking, but when we got to the right room, we found it was dirty. We called to get it serviced, then waited. Finally, the room was ready, but by then, it had taken us hours of effort to achieve success.

Problems continued throughout our stay, as we constantly had to make extra effort to get what we wanted. The first night, we went to the five-star restaurant at the hotel, checked in, got a selection of an indoor or outdoor seat, then spent forty-five minutes waiting for someone to take our drink order. To say the hotel didn't deliver on their promises would be an understatement. At the end of the trip, I wrote a letter to the hotel and described everything that went wrong.

I never expected to hear back from the hotel, but I was wrong. The general manager reached out to me and apologized for the experience, offering a complimentary vacation so I could experience just how good the hotel could be.

We accepted the offer and went back to the hotel. To be fair, things were better this time, but we had problems. For example, they had moved the entrance of the hotel, but they still hadn't updated the directions. This is perhaps the most basic touchpoint of all—customers have to be able to actually get to your business.

CREATING HUMAN CONNECTIONS

Facilitating ease so customers can achieve success is important, but this alone doesn't create lifetime brand advocates. To do that, you have to make a human connection with your customers, and building trust is key to that process. Show that you genuinely care about them so they feel like they're doing business with real people rather than a faceless corporation. When you do that, you create memories that last a lifetime.

Not long ago, I bought a refrigerator online. I selected a delivery time on the website, but then my schedule changed. I sent the company an email and asked if it was possible to move the delivery time up a day. Because I sent the email late at night, I wasn't sure I would get a response. However, to my amazement, I not only got a response, but an actual company representative called me within minutes of me hitting send. He explained how the shipping process worked and promised to make every effort to address my need. The next morning, he called back to confirm that the delivery time had been successfully changed. This interaction proved to me that I was dealing with actual human beings who cared about their customers. The refrigerator arrived a day early, just as promised, and I continue to advocate for that store, Appliances Online, to this day, all because they created a real human connection with me and met my needs.

Bear in mind, I haven't advocated for the actual brand of the refrigerator. It's a fine product that does exactly what I need it to do, but it was the company that sold the appliance and delivered it that made the human connection.

They are the ones who earned my loyalty. People forget transactions, but they never forget the way someone made them feel. Everyone in your organization can create these touchpoints in a customer's memory in some way.

LOSING BAILEY, FINDING CARLTON

Many years ago, my godchildren purchased a soft plush bear called Bailey. When I traveled around the world, I took Bailey with me so I could photograph him in his adventures with me. I'd take pictures of him looking out hotel windows or posing in other locations throughout the hotel and send them to my godchildren.

During a stay at the Ritz-Carlton in downtown Atlanta, I returned to my room one day to find that Bailey was missing. I immediately went to the concierge and explained the situation, and within moments the staff had turned the place upside down trying to locate Bailey. Sadly, Bailey continued his vacation somewhere else in the Ritz-Carlton, or possibly at the laundry service—he might still be there to this day.

Clearly, losing this plush toy with its sentimental value was a negative experience, but what the Ritz-Carlton did next created a strong human connection that I've never forgotten. While looking for Bailey, the general manager asked me some questions about the bear. I told him the whole story about Bailey's adventures and the pictures I sent to my godchildren.

When I returned to Australia, I received a package from the Ritz-Carlton with a handwritten note from the general manager that said, "Jason, we're so sorry we couldn't locate Bailey." I had only mentioned the bear's name once or twice while talking to the general manager, but he'd made sure to remember. The note went on to say, "We hope this small gift will help you continue to share stories with your godchildren." Inside the package, I found a soft, plush tiger which I named Carlton.

Carlton has continued to accompany me on my adventures and even shared a stage with me a time or two. By paying attention and being thoughtful during a customer's moment of frustration, the staff at the Ritz-Carlton created a powerful emotional connection with me that continues to be part of my life.

This is far from the only story of the Ritz-Carlton staff creating human connections with their customers. I could share many, many examples of ways they've instilled fierce brand loyalty in me. Their staff is trained to show genuine concern and care at every level, they sustain that training with a positive culture that reinforces it and as a result they are always creating positive connections, even when something goes wrong.

DOWNSTREAM CHANGES

You can find opportunities to differentiate yourself in almost any area of your company. For example, the Australian company ME Bank had their legal team write their terms and conditions in a fun, engaging way, eliminating the legal jargon and using common language instead. By using engaging phrases, they make it simple for customers to understand what they're agreeing to. On the cover page, they've included the following amusing quote:

"I loved reading the terms & conditions!" said no one, ever."

National Australia Bank launched a new transaction feature on their ATMs in 2010. Customers can assign their favorite or most-used transaction to a single button press. Even though this made things easier, it also introduced a new friction point for customers. If someone hadn't assigned their favorite transaction, the ATM would ask them to do so every time they use the machine. A feature meant to make things easier for customers actually added an initial extra step in the process.

While trying to make things easier for your customers to achieve success, consider the impact of any changes downstream. Remember, success, ease, and connection will help drive trust when delivered consistently. Trust buys loyalty, and loyalty creates repeat and referral business.

Now I pose the following questions to you.

- When was the last time you sat down with your team and defined what success, ease, and connection look like for your customers?
- Does your team perfectly understand what you're trying to deliver to your customers?
- What are your customers' expressed and unexpressed desires?
- What could make things easier for them?
- When was the last time you empowered your team to create moments of human connection with customers?

If you've taken the time to discuss questions like these, has your team been able to deliver on success, ease, and connection in a consistent way? Are you celebrating the successes?

Chapter 5

———

SUCCESS, EASE, AND CONNECTION FOR THE EMPLOYEE

Like customers, your team members use similar lenses: success, ease, and human connection. However, what individual team members are looking for varies. For some, success is simply having a stable job. For others, it's having a clear career path to move in both horizontal and vertical directions within the organization.

MEASURING SUCCESS

Whatever their individual circumstances, employees tend to measure success according to their personal goals and their place in life. For example, one teenager might want to make some cash so they can hang out with their friends and enjoy a bit of independence from their parents. Another teenager might be saving to buy their first car. A young adult might be building a foundation for their long-term career or paying off student loan debt.

If you want to understand what success looks like for your team, take time to understand where they're coming from and what they want to achieve. If you can help them achieve success, they will be more engaged and committed to the team and the company.

During my time at Optus, we had an individual—we'll call him Brad—who applied for a job with our customer service center. At twenty years old, Brad had for a number of years been working in various positions at numerous cafés. During his interview, he highlighted his passion for delivering positive outcomes to customers. We decided he had the right attitude, and although he'd worked in a very different industry, we knew we could train him on the specific skills he needed for his role at Optus.

During the hiring process, we took the time to understand what he wanted to achieve. First, he wanted a stable job with regular hours. Later, that changed, and he wanted to expand his skills. Through mentorship and training, he was able to move to a role within operations. Today, fifteen years after he first started working for Optus, he works as a senior business analyst for a large government-owned organization, leading a large team. His current success was due in part to the fact that we took the time, as his employers, to understand what his idea of success looked like in each stage of his life.

To his credit, he took charge of his career, embraced his own personal development, and achieved success for his employer and himself, but we supported him in a way that speaks to the second lens by which team members measure experience.

EASING INTO IT

Team members like to achieve success with an amount of effort that isn't disproportionate to their idea of success. Consequently, it's not ideal to remove all hurdles to career advancement. Otherwise, you make advancement feel unsatisfying and cheap and potentially elevate team members who are underdeveloped in key skills. Instead, prune bureaucracy, removing policies that make it unnecessarily difficult for team members to achieve success.

Think about the last time you left your office at the end of a long day and felt frustrated because you'd spent the whole day trying unsuccessfully to complete a task. A whole day of spinning your wheels doesn't make you feel good about the company you work for, so as a leader, it's your job to pare back any bureaucracy that makes it harder for people to achieve their outcomes in a single day. You want people to go home with some sense of accomplishment.

When you help people go home feeling successful, it builds lifetime advocacy from those team members. Do you want a team member going home to their spouse, girlfriend or boyfriend, or housemate and complaining about how awful your company is? Of course not.

This is one of the reasons I love tools such as Agile and Lean Six Sigma: because they provide a framework for organizations to streamline processes and reduce errors so team members achieve more. When you can help team members be more efficient, you open up more time and opportunity for them to connect with customers. Ideally, you're not simply motivating employees to do a better job, but you're also helping to sustain a positive outward focus.

Remember, your goal is to maintain a dual focus on both employee and customer experience. Any process that doesn't contribute to the success of both should be eliminated, unless it's a regulatory requirement.

When I was asked to work at the call center in Telstra, the company at the time required team members to systematically follow every step in a convoluted process when dealing with a customer. No steps could be eliminated under any circumstances. This might not have been a problem if there had been only a few steps, but call center staff had almost two hundred steps they had to follow. Each team member kept a binder on their desk with elaborate screenshots for every single step. It was cumbersome and decimated efficiency, so I knew we had to change it. Using Six Sigma methodology, which helps eliminate defects and waste from any process, we were able to pare down the steps to eighty.

Team members were now able to solve problems faster and give individual customers more focus and attention. Interactions improved, and employees felt more satisfied with work. Customers got their product delivered with a higher level of attentiveness, which made them feel more valued.

When was the last time you reviewed your processes to ensure bureaucracy was minimized so team members could make connections faster? Are team members taking unnecessary steps to complete a transaction? Are any steps of your process present only for the sake of the process?

You might consider assigning someone to become the so-called chief bureaucracy buster on your team, critically analyzing every step of your processes to see which ones can be eliminated. Whether you use Six Sigma, Lean, or some other methodology, make sure you are constantly working to streamline processes so your team can focus their energy on customer interactions.

You want to make sure employees are on *purpose* instead of merely on *task*. Disneyland's purpose includes creating happiness for park visitors. As a member of the janitorial staff, a team member's task is to help keep the theme park clean and attractive for guests, but their purpose is to create happiness. Therefore, if they see an opportunity to provide assistance to a guest, they are empowered by the company to go off-task in order to make the most of that opportunity.

Are you creating an environment that enables your team members to focus on what matters most?

Remember, it's not a score. It's a real human connection.

LEADERS WHO GENUINELY CARE

After success and ease, the third way team members measure their experience is through connection. They want to see that leaders genuinely care and show interest in them. Manipulating emotions to get employees to do what you want isn't connection. Real connection is about understanding what makes them tick, why they work for you, and how their work integrates into their lives.

Many organizations use employee engagement surveys to gauge how well they're doing, but the week before they send out the survey, they spend time communicating all the great things they do for team members. This is an attempt to manipulate the score, but we shouldn't be focusing on a score anyway. Rather, we should focus on showing team members that we genuinely care and want to help them live their best lives while being part of our organization.

When was the last time you asked employees for feedback on how their day was going? When was the last time you asked them at the end of the day how you could make tomorrow even better?

If you provide easy avenues for your team members to provide feedback about how their day or week is going, over time you will have a cumulative amount of data providing key insights on areas that cause stress or delight for your team. Of course, if you intend to seek employee feedback often, make sure you set clear expectations with your team members about what is going to be done with that feedback. Clarify how often it will be reviewed, how quickly, and how it might influence decisions the business makes. Whether you collect employee feedback every day, once a month, or once a year, your team members should have a clear understanding of how those data drive changes in the organization.

Some companies take the approach, "Leave your personal life at the door." I believe that's impossible. Nobody can ever fully compartmentalize their work life and personal life. Instead, I strongly encourage leaders to integrate their organization into the overall life of each employee, making the team an extension of where they live, work, and play. That makes employees feel like the company has their best interests at heart.

At one organization I worked for, managers gave team members handwritten birthday and anniversary-of-employment cards. Eventually, we stopped that activity because we thought it was a waste of time. When the annual employee survey went out, we learned that many people were unhappy that we'd stopped. Even though it was a small gesture, it showed people that management cared about them as people.

If you've ever visited a Disney park or stayed at a Disney resort, you might have noticed that every employee (or as Disney calls them, cast member) has a name tag with their hometown on it. This creates an immediate opportunity for a human connection from team member to team member. If one team member notices that another employee's name tag says, "Sydney, Australia," they can ask questions about their hometown and what it's like to live there. It also allows customers to connect with cast members, bringing the real person into what could otherwise be merely a professional interaction.

When was the last time you asked employees how the organization fits into their wider life? What are some simple ways you could get feedback from employees in real time? Many companies, online and in person, offer simple ways for customers to give instant feedback, such as clicking on a one-to-five-star rating or selecting an appropriate emoji face. Could you do something similar at the exit door so employees could rate their day before they head home?

I'm not suggesting you should chase a score every day, but regular and real-time (or close-to-real-time) feedback enables you to systematically review the key drivers of motivation or demotivation and make improvements based on those insights. In other words, use the data over time to identify what works well and leverage that, minimizing the behaviors or actions that disengage team members.

Real-time feedback builds better connections with your team and transforms them into brand advocates. When an employee is socializing with friends or family and someone says, "Your company is bad," they will feel proud to defend the company and help that disgruntled customer achieve the success they're looking for.

Chapter 6

———

MEASURING EXPERIENCE AS A COMPANY

Measuring experience as a company is absolutely essential for improving the experience of both team members and customers. All too often, I see companies surveying simply for the sake of surveying. By that, I mean many companies collect lots of data through surveys and then do nothing with the data. They don't turn insight into action.

In almost every industry these days, we receive requests to complete surveys or are provided avenues to provide feedback. I've even seen requests for feedback in airport and shopping mall bathrooms. Feedback is crucial to every business because it help leaders identify areas of both success and opportunity.

When done right, it helps you get a clear sense of the human impact of your customer and employee interactions. However, it's important to remember that both customers and employees expect negative feedback to result in some kind of substantive improvement. If you don't have the organizational capacity to act on the results of a particular feedback question, don't ask that question until you do.

Respect customers' and employees' time by keeping survey length aligned with your ability to turn the insights into action to improve the business. This ensures team members won't be swamped in a sea of data. It's better if they can be laser-focused to spot the hidden gems in feedback that will drive experience improvements.

Showing appreciation for your customers is a foundational aspect of experience, and one way you can show appreciation is to avoid over surveying them. Limit customer feedback to insights that will lead to action, because, after all, knowledge without action is useless. Taking action on feedback is, of course, another important way to show appreciation.

MEANINGFUL MEASUREMENTS

There are a number of ways organizations measure customer experience. Many of them measure satisfaction, which occurs when a customer or employee is able to achieve success with the amount of effort they expected to expend. Of course, if you can't satisfy your customers, you will have a very hard time building brand loyalty, but satisfaction is only one element of experience. If you measure only this one thing, you won't get a clear picture of how you're doing.

To obtain a meaningful measurement of customer experience, you can use the following forms of feedback.

CUSTOMER/EMPLOYEE EFFORT SCORE

A customer effort score contains questions about the amount of effort it took customers to have their issue resolved. It's best done immediately after a transaction or interaction with a customer. The longer you wait and the further the customer gets from the interaction, the less meaningful the data become. You want an immediate emotional response so you can act on it as needed.

Employee effort scores have also been gaining traction in certain companies. For example, a company might ask their employees, "Is it easy to perform your tasks? Are company processes simplified and streamlined?" For customers, "Was it easy to achieve XYZ?"

Remember, if you're going to ask specific questions

about the amount of effort expended by customers and employees, your team must be ready to take that insight and act on it. Otherwise, the feedback does you no good. Also, make sure you're not asking the same people the same questions over and over without demonstrating that you've made improvements, or you will erode trust. People will start to think, "They never listen to us anyway, so why provide feedback?"

You can't address every piece of feedback, of course, or focus everyone into making every single improvement that is ever recommended. Instead, you are looking for common problems that are mentioned by multiple people and focusing your effort on addressing those.

Ask a specific question for a month or two, then collect the insights, form action plans, and implement changes. Let customers see and experience the improvements, then reintroduce the effort score survey to see if results change.

I recommend looking at the top three issues that will have the greatest impact, but ideally those issues that are cross-divisional. The more you can work on resolving issues that require cross-divisional collaboration, the faster you will reinforce that customer and employee experience requires the relentless focus of everyone.

Net Promoter Score (NPS) was created by Bain & Company to measure the likelihood of a customer referring your company. It's widely used in every industry as a way of measuring customer loyalty. Respondents are asked to measure their likelihood of recommending the company, on a scale of zero to ten. Someone who selects a score of nine or ten is considered a promoter, meaning they actively encourage other people to utilize your brand. People who select a score between zero and six are considered detractors, meaning they discourage others from doing business with you during conversations around the dinner table or water cooler. A score of seven or eight is considered neutral, a respondent who is neither overwhelmed nor underwhelmed. They have no strong bond with your brand, but they haven't developed a dislike for you either.

To arrive at your NPS, the percentage of detractors is subtracted from the percentage of promoters to arrive at a number somewhere between -100 and 100. The higher the resulting number, the more likely it is that customers and employees are actively recommending you to others.

NPS can be applied to either a transactional survey or a brand health survey. The former measures the likelihood of getting a recommendation immediately after a transaction has taken place, while the latter measures the likelihood of a recommendation taking place after some time has passed. This gives you a clear indication of the power of your brand by revealing how customers react to you immediately and how strongly you linger in their minds.

Some individuals in your business may challenge the NPS methodology. I have heard people in many companies say that NPS is unfair because responses of seven and eight aren't counted in promoter percentages. However, I encourage you not to modify the NPS methodology. In every industry, companies that have implemented NPS without alteration of the calculation method have had greater success in building a consistent focus on improving experiences and growing customer loyalty, employee engagement, and profitability.

The risk of a measurement like NPS, Customer Effort Score and others is that they can create a culture where people are chasing a score rather than creating connections with customers and employees. In my opinion, the power is not in the score but in the reason behind the score. I recommend providing respondents with the opportunity to explain their reasoning so you can improve the experience.

There's also employee Net Promoter Score (eNPS), which measures the likelihood that employees would recommend your company as a place to work. Rarely will someone recommend a workplace that they find overly bureaucratic, lacking structure, or unsupportive.

Using NPS in tandem with eNPS can give you a clear picture of your company's health. As long as you allow respondents to explain their scores, you will see areas of needed improvement. As you make adjustments and increase those scores, you should see a reduction in both staff and customer turnover, resulting in a lower cost to serve and an increase in company performance.

WORD-OF-MOUTH INDEX

A more recent measurement that is growing in popularity is called the Word-of-Mouth Index (WoMI). It was originally developed by the CX research company ForeSee. A question specific to WoMI is, "How likely are you to use the product or service in the future?"

This provides another way to measure the health of your brand, and the end result is presented as a percentage. WoMI is an additional tool you can add to your kit when working to improve customer experience.

I don't think it necessarily matters which measurement methodology you use, but I strongly encourage you not to switch measurement approaches too often. You need a baseline of data that you can improve on and compare to regularly. People need to understand your methodology, so choose one, embed it, and stick with it until it no longer proves useful for driving the company forward.

PLATFORM SOFTWARE

One of the first things you should do when working to improve customer and employee experience is to invest in an experience management platform that can solicit feedback in real time (or near real time) and further out.

Be sure to provide respondents with a way to give feedback with actual stories. Once the data begin to come in, share the stories rather than the scores. Let direct feedback drive your improvements, and always celebrate positive feedback and recommendations. In the organizations I've worked for, I've always made sure to share verbatim quotes from customer and employee feedback on posters or flash them on TV screens, along with the score for context.

Over the years, I've looked at a number of systems, and my recommendation is to use a software-as-a-service (SaaS), cloud-based solution that offers the flexibility to create, deploy, manage, and scale voice-of-customer (or employee) surveys. Companies such as Qualtrics provide class-leading flexible cloud-based solutions, so you can put your touchpoint, brand health, product, and employee surveys in one place. This enables you to connect the dots between key data so you can build out your programs and share feedback widely with your team. One of the reasons I advocate cloud-based solutions is because you can usually benefit from new enhancements and capabilities as they are developed, without needing to invest huge amounts to gain innovation and capability on an in-house system.

Other commonly used voice-of-customer or survey platforms for large companies include MaritzCX, Medallia, Satmetrix, and InMoment. I encourage you not to wait for your company or team to gain access to these enterprise-grade platforms. Platforms such as Delighted and AskNicely provide you with quick solutions that are easy and fast to implement so you can start gathering feedback. Systems such as Delighted and AskNicely can be set up and deployed in minutes.

A key feature I look for in the platforms I use is their flexibility in how customers receive invitations to participate and how you can share results. Some people love getting information by email, others prefer text message, and some enjoy logging into a dashboard. You need a system that will engage the largest cross-section of stakeholders.

I recommend sending a text message to your team every

day with one detractor comment and one promoter comment to keep them focused on people rather than scores. Furthermore, companies such as LivingLens, who integrate with the Qualtrics platform, provide a way for customers and employees to send video feedback from their smartphone or computer, which provides another way to bring the real people out from behind the numbers, so you can connect with individuals.

Ultimately, it doesn't matter which of these platforms or measuring programs you use, so long as you can translate the resulting data into insights that drive action. Insight without action is like a pool without water: useless!

—

PART III

HOW TO BUILD AN EXPERIENCE STRATEGY

You understand the importance of customer and employee experience for your business, but it's equally important for your own career. You could become famous just by leading a team obsessed with delivering the greatest experience to both internal and external customers.

In the next section, I will provide practical advice to help you accelerate the experience that your company and team deliver. We will discuss key elements to begin improving that experience, and I will give you the information you need to define and implement an effective experience strategy.

As you probably know from your own interactions as an employee and customer, expectations change over time. For this reason, I can't provide you with a silver bullet to immediately solve all problems. Instead, you need to build an experience strategy that can evolve, staying slightly ahead of customer expectations. As long as you deliver an experience that is slightly better than expectations, you will continue to build lifelong loyalty and brand advocates.

Chapter 7

THREE KEY ELEMENTS OF EVERYONE'S EXPERIENCE JOURNEY

Throughout my career, whether working in the banking industry, government, retail, automotive, or the non-profit sector, I have observed three common elements in every employee and customer journey. These elements, clearly defined, understood, and consistently carried out by all team members, lay the foundation for meaningful differentiation.

The first element is the way you *welcome or greet* customers and employees. The second is how you *interact and guide* them. The third is how you *show gratitude and appreciation*. When you make customers and employees feel welcome, provide easy guidance, and show genuine appreciation for their time, business, or work, you create a solid basis for a sustainable experience.

THE WIN STRATEGY

To improve the experience your team delivers, start by clearly identifying those three key elements of every customer interaction: *greeting, guiding,* and *showing appreciation*. Do they feel welcome? Do you interact with them to provide easy guidance? Do you show genuine appreciation? By focusing on these easy-to-grasp concepts, you can begin to build momentum, which is perhaps the most important aspect of any experience strategy.

When I worked for Target, my team launched what we called the WIN strategy: Welcome, Interact, No queues. We wanted to win with every customer, welcoming them into our stores, interacting with them by guiding them to their destination, and making it easy for them to navigate our retail footprint. You might say, "Where's appreciation in that strategy?" I would reply that appreciation and gratitude begin by not making customers wait to complete their purchase.

If you've been to Target, you know they do have queues from time to time, so we weren't pretending to have done away with them entirely. Instead, our strategy addressed what to do when a queue started to form. We wanted to avoid a situation where a customer approached the open registers, saw a line at each one, and said, "Why do they have only a few registers open?" This is a common friction point in retail stores, so we wanted to remove it.

Everyone on the team knew our goal was to minimize queues, so if all open registers were full, team members would instinctively manage the queues. First, they interacted with and engaged customers. Then, as soon as a register opened, they would guide customers there. At the register, team members would then acknowledge the customer's wait and thank them. It was an easy improvement that every team member could understand. They greeted customers, interacted with them throughout the purchasing cycle to make it easier, and expressed appreciation.

Of course, the type of welcome you give differs depending on your organization. At a retail store, a welcome might literally mean stationing someone at the entrance to say, "Welcome to Target," to every customer who enters. Don't overthink the verbiage of your greeting. Just make sure to use words everyone can understand. A welcome might also mean providing a catalog of products and directing customers to promotional items, so they can find what they want more easily. When you are readily available to help customers, it makes them feel welcomed at your store, which helps to build trust.

Interaction is about allowing team members to go off-task in order to help customers achieve success. At Target, even if a team member was assigned to hang clothes or pack shelves, they were expected to help customers. When they saw a customer, they were expected to make eye contact and greet them. If a customer needed assistance, the team member assisted them, even if it meant interrupting their assigned task. We needed our team members to be on purpose first, task second. When a customer asked for the location of a specific product, the team member was to provide clear directions and then offer to take them there.

Of course, some customers don't want a store worker to figuratively hold their hand and lead them to their destination. They want to feel empowered to go there on their own, but the offer demonstrates that the team member wants to make it easy for them. Just make sure they can also say no easily. Never pressure a customer to receive what they might not want.

The relentless focus on improving customer experience at Target caused the company to win the Discount Department Store of the Year award from Roy Morgan in 2015.[15]

15   Roy Morgan, "Roy Morgan Customer Satisfaction Awards: Announcing Australia's Retail Superstars," February 19, 2015, accessed August 14, 2018, http://www.roymorgan.com/findings/6072-retail-winners-customer-satisfaction-201502182343.

With these three elements—*greeting, guiding*, and *showing appreciation*—you empower customers to achieve success with less effort and a strong sense of connection. This might not sound like groundbreaking stuff, and I agree. Greeting, guiding, and showing appreciation aren't groundbreaking, but the magic is that everyone understands what they mean, which makes it easier to deliver an amazing experience consistently.

You must pursue these things with relentless passion, empowering your team and giving them the tools they need, setting clear expectations about what you expect to see in each of these three areas. Each time you deliver on the three elements consistently, you create proof points that build trust.

CREATE A DUMMY GUIDE

The first thing you should do is sit down, either alone or with your team, and create a dummy guide for these three elements. What should a greeting or welcome in your organization look like? If you're an online-only business, that means looking at your landing page: does it make people feel welcome? In regard to your contact center, do customers feel welcome when they call, or do they feel like they have to go through ten layers of automated questions before they achieve success? Write down your answers.

When it comes to guiding customers, make it as easy as possible for them to achieve success. Whether you're an online business or a traditional retail store, you absolutely must have a website these days. Is your website easy to navigate? Can your customers easily get where they want to go?

How often have you heard that your first impression is the most important? While the first impression certainly sets the mood for what comes next, the last moment of an interaction is just as important. Showing gratitude or appreciation is a nice way to close an interaction, even if the customer didn't purchase anything. Even if they only spent time researching your products, you should still be thankful.

In your dummy guide, describe what that thankfulness looks like. At Target, it was the combination of reducing or eliminating queues combined with a friendly, "Thank you for shopping at Target." Team members were empowered to use the language they felt most comfortable with, so the expression of gratitude felt more natural. You don't want appreciation to sound false or scripted. Speak in a way that sounds genuine and do it regularly.

NO NEED FOR THEATRICS

Of course, greeting, guiding, and showing genuine appreciation come in many forms. Consider the example of Hong Ha, a Vietnamese bakery in Sydney. For more than thirty years, they've been selling Vietnamese baked goods, but they actually have fewer than fifteen items on their menu, all of which are variations of one another. With this simple menu and an unassuming storefront, they get customers lining up outside of the business all day long from open to close.

I've been there in the mornings, at lunch, and at almost every other time and had to stand in a line that winds outside the store and up the sidewalk. It's quite an experience, especially when you realize that there's another Vietnamese bakery a hundred feet down the road that has no queue. In fact, I've never seen more than a single customer at a time in the other bakery.

The staff at Hong Ha don't depend on theatrics or hype in the way they greet people, guide them, or show appreciation, but they are absolutely consistent. Every customer is greeted in the same way. Every customer is asked the same questions to guide them through the purchase process. Every customer, after being served, is given a polite goodbye. They combine this with a consistent delivery of their product.

People don't always queue up because there's a marching band or a big presentation. Sometimes they queue up because they want 100 percent consistency in experience and product. It goes to show how absolutely vital it is to get consistency right. Understand the fundamentals—*success*, *ease*, and the *human connection*—and consistently couple them with *greeting, guiding*, and showing *genuine appreciation*. Sometimes that's all it takes to stand out from your competition.

THE DIGITAL WORLD

As our world becomes more digital, there's a need to translate greeting, guiding, and genuine appreciation into the digital world. At a recent conference, I participated in a panel discussion with a representative from UBank, a subsidiary of National Australia Bank that is entirely digital. They've deployed AI software to help customers complete online mortgage applications. If you've ever gone through the mortgage application process, you know how difficult some of the questions can be, even during your second mortgage. By making it easier for customers to successfully complete their loan applications, UBank is also achieving success by receiving more applications that are correctly filled out.

Many customers abandon the online loan process because of the difficulty, but UBank is eliminating this friction point. It's a great example of how a business focused on guiding customers and making it easier for them to achieve success is also creating a win for themselves. By taking the time to understand the key friction points for the customer, UBank was able to create an easier online application process, resulting in a 15 percent increase in the conversion rate.

Customer and employee experience isn't about customers and employees winning at the expense of the company. When done right, everyone wins, because when you focus on the customer, you improve your business metrics.

CREATING CONNECTIONS THROUGH APPRECIATION

While working on this book, I spoke to Nienke Bloem, a leading customer experience professional based in the Netherlands. During our conversation, she shared a great example of how a company showing appreciation to its customers creates a strong connection with them. While traveling on Emirates airline, she was rewarded with a free upgrade to first class.

It was an unexpected surprise, but the takeaway from this story isn't that you have to give customers free upgrades to deliver a great experience. That's not what experiences are about, and it's not even the wow moment of the story. As Nienke took her seat, the flight attendant noticed how excited she was. In conversation, Nienke mentioned that it was her first time in an Emirates first-class suite and that she couldn't imagine spending the money herself for first class. "This is probably the only time I'll get to enjoy it," she said.

The flight attendant went to the galley and came back with a Polaroid instant camera. She took a picture of Nienke in her suite and gave it to her so she would have a photo of her experience. As it turns out, Emirates has designed this into their process as a way to show gratitude, and they've trained their teams on how to use the Polaroid to create a connection with a customer.

You might wonder, "Why not just take a picture with a smartphone?" How many pictures do you have on your smartphone? Most people have dozens, if not thousands, so the picture would have been lost in the mix. Creating a Polaroid gave Nienke a unique souvenir. While a smartphone picture would have been easy to share on social media, the Polaroid has become a real conversation starter. She keeps it on her desk to this day and likes to share the story with people. It's a powerful moment that still resonates in her memory.

I challenge you to find ways to build appreciation into your processes and training. Provide tools, like Emirates did with the Polaroid, to help your team show genuine appreciation while creating connections with customers.

WELCOME TO THE TEAM

Employee experience contains the same three key elements. How do you *greet* them? How do you *guide* them? How do you *show appreciation* for the work they do? If you apply these elements to your recruiting and onboarding processes and make them part of your work environment and how you lead your teams, it will set you apart from other employers, but the keys are consistency and simplification.

When recruiting a new team member, companies often send a letter of congratulations for signing the contract, but what if the manager also sent a handwritten note saying, "Welcome to the team. I look forward to your first day, and I can't wait to celebrate the many successes you will achieve."

I've done something similar for almost every employee I've ever hired, and in every instance, the employees who received a handwritten note showed up for work the first day with more passion and excitement than those who didn't. It's a way to start the welcoming process before they even walk through the door, and it makes a tremendous impact.

Think about how your company welcomes employees on their first day. Do you greet them at reception? Does someone guide them to the lift? Is their desk already put together and ready to go? Of course, making someone feel welcome doesn't end after their first day on the job. Your employees should feel welcome every day. I'm not suggesting you stand at reception every morning and shake every hand. That's not practical, but you can design the parking lot and employee entrance to feel welcoming by making them look *just as nice as the customer entrance*. Why do we often relegate employees to poorly lit parking lots in the back, ask them to walk through a nondescript door into an ugly back hallway? Shouldn't they, too, feel great arriving at the building?

John Deere does a great job of making every team member feel welcome. The very first email a new John Deere employee receives is from the CEO, and it contains a video explaining the history and legacy that makes the company famous. How much nicer is that single personalized email from the CEO than simply being added to a company-wide distribution list and receiving a plethora of impersonal messages?

Interacting with employees isn't simply about conversations or messages. It's also about how easy it is for employees to understand their pay slips or access information on the intranet. Do you invest as much energy and effort in designing the intranet as you do the customer website? If not, why not? Do you show appreciation when someone does a great job? You don't have to buy expensive gifts. Sometimes, just taking the time to say thank you is enough.

TRAINING FOR CONSISTENCY

Flight Centre Travel Group is Australia's largest retail travel outlet and one of the world's largest travel agency groups, spanning more than ninety countries and employing almost twenty thousand people. If you walk into any Flight Centre store, you'll have the same experience every time. They've nailed consistency. They interact with customers very well, guiding them to fulfill both expressed and unexpressed travel desires. You can book a no-frills "point A to point B" trip, or they'll help you book your flight, accommodations, rental car, tour guides, and activities all at once. No matter how basic or how complex your travel plans, employees put the same amount of care into every interaction.

They always ask the right questions so they can clarify what a customer is trying to achieve. For example, you might walk in and tell them you want a round-trip ticket from Los Angeles to San Francisco, and they will figure out what you're trying to achieve and make suggestions to ease the process, such as booking a car service from the airport to your home or finding the most affordable options for a short beach trip. Yes, they will try to upsell you but always in gentle, helpful ways, and a no never offends. Ultimately, they come up with ideas that match your goal, and their priority is to understand your needs and deliver success.

I worked at Flight Centre for a short time, and I clearly remember the training process. We were trained to interact with customers, create an experience for them, and connect with them to create long-lasting memories. How did Flight Centre become a $20 billion business despite competing with the likes of Expedia, Kayak, and TripAdvisor? They've endured the test of time because they find ways to interact with customers consistently and deliver solutions in seamless ways. That consistency delivers on one of the most powerful human emotions—the emotion of trust. Do they show gratitude? Absolutely. It's not uncommon for your travel associate to check in with you near the end of your trip to make sure everything went well. It's how they build loyalty and advocacy.

CONNECTING WITH THE BRAND

Warby Parker is known for disrupting the way people buy prescription glasses and sunglasses, offering customers the option to try five frames in the comfort of their homes before deciding which one to buy. They also offer competitive prices, but you don't disrupt an industry purely on product or price. You do it with experience, and Warby

Parker understands that the experience you create for your employees will ultimately impact your customers.

At Warby Parker, every employee is welcomed in a way that connects them with the origins of the brand. It starts with a welcome gift, a copy of Jack Kerouac's *The Dharma Bums*, because the company's name is inspired by characters in the book. Employees also get Martin's handmade pretzels from the Union Square Greenmarket, because the company founders used to buy them to snack on during the startup days (read: early mornings and late nights).

It doesn't end there. Every new employee also gets a pair of glasses for themselves and one for a friend. What a great way to make sure employees experience the product and recommend them! They bake it into their onboarding process.

WHAT IS YOUR COMPANY FAMOUS FOR?

When I worked at Target in Australia, they held an annual event called the Greatest Toy Sale on Earth. It was held in the middle of the year in order to guarantee the lowest prices in the nation. Families would line up until midnight outside the stores to be the first ones to get limited-release products or to acquire the "must-have" toy of the year for Christmas. Every register was open, and queues would often run the length of the store, with some customers waiting almost an hour to get served.

This event reinforced the importance of interacting with customers and showing appreciation while they wait in a long queue. Other stores had similar sales, but we kept getting positive reviews, while they received mostly negative reviews. The difference wasn't queue length. Instead, the positive reviews spoke about the friendliness of staff. Competing stores had great prices, but they left people alone while they waited at the register.

At Target, we thanked people, passed out lollipops, and gave them estimates of how much longer their wait might be. Once a customer got close to a register, staff would start taking clothes off hangers to expedite checkout. After a while, customers noticed team members removing hangers and started to copy them, so team members began collecting hangers and thanking customers instead. We were removing friction points and turning them into opportunities to connect with people, and it made a difference. Customers would share on social media how fun and easy the experience was.

Ask yourself, what do you want your company to become famous for?

Zappos's amazing growth is, in large part, a direct result

of their interactions with employees. From day one, they set up employees for success, and they continue this throughout their time at the company. The onboarding process is intense and detailed, because they want to delight employees as much as employees delight customers. Getting a job at Zappos isn't easy, but if you get hired and decide within the first four weeks that it was a mistake, you can opt out of the job and they will pay you $2,000 to leave.

Employees who haven't even worked four weeks at the company can walk away with $2,000! That might sound crazy, but it's actually a radical way of showing appreciation. Ultimately, that money is paid back tenfold by the customers who weren't made unhappy by a disgruntled employee who stuck around because they couldn't afford to leave.

Zappos is famous around the world for their best practices in customer service, yet they sell only in the United States. By delivering an experience that turns employees into fans who are highly engaged with the purpose of the company, they are able to deliver a consistent experience for their customers.

A SIMPLE GESTURE

What are you doing this week to clearly define the three

elements—greeting, guidance, appreciation—for your customers and team members? How easy would it be if everyone on your team understood what *great* meant for each of them?

Let me encourage you, after you finish this chapter (or now), to sit down and handwrite a note to a customer or team member, expressing appreciation for their business or the work they do. Handwrite their name and address on the envelope as well. Even if you have terrible handwriting, do it. It takes only a few moments, but there's tremendous power in this simple gesture.

Why not an email? Simple. Look at your inbox. How many emails do you get in a single day? Fifteen years ago, it was common to get tons of regular mail, including a lot of personal correspondence. These days, mailboxes mostly contain advertisements and the occasional bill. To receive a handwritten letter in the mail today really hits home in a personal way. You don't have to write a novel. Three simple sentences will suffice.

Isn't it every marketer's dream to cut through the noise and be heard? If you're the only personalized letter in someone's mailbox, you're cutting through in a dramatic way. Take a moment right now to do this before continuing on with the book.

Chapter 8

FIND YOUR EXPERIENCE PRINCIPLES

Procrastination is the enemy of action, and distraction is procrastination in disguise. I encourage every experience professional to focus on building momentum in their experience strategy rather than trying to find the one silver bullet that will fix everything.

Customer and employee experience as a discipline has been growing in popularity in recent years, and with that popularity comes a wealth of books, software, conferences, and exercises such as journey mapping. Many of these can become distractions, preventing you from taking action as you search for your silver bullet. It's great to listen and learn, gathering ideas and concepts, but if you're not careful, they can get you off focus. Try a simple Google search for "improve experience" and see how many responses you get. You can get lost in that sea of distractions.

There's nothing wrong with journey mapping or other exercises, but you don't have to learn how to journey map before you can start improving experience. (Of course, you may find journey mapping a useful tool, but don't get hung up on it or any tool before starting.) Focus on your strategy and start taking steps to achieve it. Don't let anything draw your attention away from consistently improving.

ESTABLISH YOUR PRINCIPLES

Maybe you're not sure what your starting point should be. What's the first action you should take in implementing a strategy to improve customer and employee experience? I recommend you begin by developing your experience principles, which are the things you want your business to consistently deliver to customers and employees. Your principles should guide all aspects of your organization.

When I attended Ashton Media's Customer 360 Symposium, I had the opportunity to listen to Ingrid Purcell, chief experience officer of ME Bank. ME Bank refers to their customer experience principles as "customer promises," and she describes them as follows:

- Know me.
- Know more than me.
- Don't bullshit me.
- Make me smile.

To create a culture built around these things, Ingrid said they regularly ask employees, "How are you living the customer promises?" This single question breaks down bureaucracy and maintains a laser focus on delivering what matters most.

Do you know your customers? Do you know more about your products than they do so you can help them make informed decisions? Are you giving them the facts rather than bullshit? Are you making them smile through friendly interactions?

In an ideal world, your experience principles should be applied equally to both employees and customers. They should be easy to understand and relatable. Whether you call them "principles," "promises," or something else, make sure they're clear enough so every member of your team can understand them.

I recommend having no more than three to five principles to ensure people can easily recall and live them. These aren't things to post on the wall so employees can walk by and ignore them. Experience principles should drive people to act in a certain way, and they should be relevant for every customer and employee.

At Telstra, we had five customer experiences. One of them was "Know who I am." It worked for every customer, whether they were an individual consumer, the owner of a small business, or part of a huge multinational organization. Any employee serving a customer can understand what "know who I am" means and apply it in every interaction. Each business unit might have a different example of what the principle looks like in action, but the principle itself never changes.

At Optus, their enduring tag line is "Yes, Optus," a principle born out of the idea of challenging the status quo. In practice, it meant saying yes more often than saying no. While it wasn't called an experience principle, it was articulated in the same way. Presented as a question for employees, it became, "How can you say yes to a customer?" Of course, we couldn't say yes to every customer request, but the mission was to find a way if at all possible. It drove every interaction and helped everyone maintain focus on finding solutions that would deliver success for customers.

DRIVERS OF SATISFACTION AND DISSATISFACTION

Is there something like the yes principle you could deploy

in your organization to differentiate? This isn't merely a marketing gimmick. When you set a principle, you establish expectations, and the moment you fail to deliver, you start destroying trust. Without trust, customers will never feel connected to your brand and employees will never feel connected to the company. Without trust, loyalty can't exist.

If you were to ask five of your employees today, "What promise do we make to our team?" would you get five different, possibly incompatible, answers? The principles you set define experience in your organization, and they prevent employees from having divergent ideas of what you mean.

When establishing your experience principles, gather the feedback you've collected from customers and employees. Look for the moments that created joy or excitement in your organization. What are the interactions that people commonly refer to when praising the company? Narrow this down to a top ten list of what we'll call "drivers of satisfaction."

It's a good idea to do the same thing for the drivers of dissatisfaction. What are the top ten negative interactions mentioned most often in feedback? Find connecting threads between your two lists to help you identify which drivers are the most powerful.

Let me give you a practical example.

When reviewing your customer feedback, you might find that a majority of your promoters mention things such as knowledge. At the same time, your detractors might say things like, "The consultant had no knowledge about the features; I had to do my own research." This gives you a clear indication of the power of knowledge to your customers. If you can increase the knowledge of your team members and help them turn it into value for customers, you have the makings of a great experience principle.

Once you have analyzed your drivers of satisfaction and dissatisfaction, you can create your initial list of experience principles. Take the list to your marketing, public relations, and human resources teams and get feedback. Ask the critical question, "If we consistently delivered on these, would it make us stand out from our competitors?"

Refine your experience list and present it to your C-suite and ask them, "Would you want your business to be famous for these three to five principles?" If the principles resonate with your executive leaders, then you've successfully taken your first step toward implementing an experience strategy.

Don't worry if the principles you set today will be the principles you have five years from now. Customer and employee expectations change over time, so it's a good idea to periodically review your experience principles. However, don't try to change them every year. Like any good strategy, they need time to be accepted and become embedded in every level of your organization.

Chapter 9

KNOW THE PROCESS AND THE PRODUCT

Experience principles provide the basis for a laser-like focus on the core elements of what your brand, team, or organization will become famous for. One experience principle I recommend all companies have is, "Know your process and products." This principle is about getting the fundamentals right, having the knowledge you need to help customers and employees achieve success, and doing so with repeatability and consistency.

These days, people have such a wealth of information at their fingertips through Google and various information-sharing platforms, but information alone isn't of any value if it can't be turned into application. It's good to know the features of a particular product, but if you can't articulate how to use those features, what use is the information?

Team members must know how to apply information about processes and products in order to deliver consistently on expectations. However, being consistent is only the beginning. Team members must be able to apply their knowledge to help customers leverage and realize the full value of the product or services they are purchasing.

Invest in ongoing training and skills development. It doesn't have to be expensive. Sometimes an investment in training and skills development is simply an investment of time. You can start today.

GETTING THE BASICS RIGHT

I first learned about Magic Castle Hotel in Los Angeles through the book *The Power of Moments* by Chip and Dan Heath. At the time of writing this book, Magic Castle is rated the number three hotel in LA on TripAdvisor. It's not trying to be the next Ritz-Carlton or Four Seasons. If you look at the photos online, you won't be wowed by the premium finishes or the exclusivity of the property. In fact, some people might be turned off by its glorious yellow paint job. However, Magic Castle delivers a memorable experience.

The key to the hotel's success is getting the basics right. If they didn't get their processes and products right, nobody would care about the more unique and unusual activities at the hotel, such as the Popsicle Hotline (look it up). In a similar way, nobody would care if a hotel offered the most expensive and luxurious bed if the staff never took time to clean the room. If you don't meet the standard, nothing else matters, so you have to get your processes right and deliver your products as promised. To do that, your team needs to clearly understand them both.

When I first went to work for Optus, my team served twenty-four corporate clients, and those clients' needs were not being met. One of the first things I did was to create bite-sized knowledge and information sessions for team members across all disciplines. From customer service inquiries to billing to product service, we improved process and product knowledge for all team members.

Within ninety days of implementing these information sessions and helping the team apply their knowledge to customer interactions, we were able to meet every key performance indicator, not only internally but for each individual customer. It was the first time the Optus team had met those expectations in years, and it increased customer satisfaction and advocacy by double digits.

I've applied the "know the process and products" principle in almost every role where I've had to improve the performance of my team. At Fairfax Media, one of Australia's largest independent media companies, I guided the organization through the process of outsourcing their contact centers to a third-party provider in the Philippines, New Zealand, and the United States. To ensure our team in Manila and our other locations knew exactly what to do and say in every customer interaction, we ensured that training programs continued beyond the initial four-week induction program. We reinforced process and product knowledge, first making sure our team could deliver on fundamentals, then helping them to develop a strong rapport with customers.

The vast majority of team members had never worked in the media industry before, so they didn't even know the difference between a display advertisement and a classified advertisement. We had our work cut out for us, and we knew that until they got the fundamentals right, we couldn't move into creating lifetime loyalty. Once the team had mastered the fundamentals and were consistently able to seamlessly deliver the products customers wanted, we worked on building advocacy and brand loyalty.

If you have a product that is better experienced than explained, consider ways you can get your team to experience it. For example, if you sell mobile phones, make sure team members play around with the latest model. If you sell websites, like GoDaddy, consider giving each employee the ability to create a website for internal use.

The idea is to engage your team in a fun way to make them enthusiastic about the product.

An example of this can be found at Disney. They have their food and beverage teams regularly host dinners for new recruits, which allows recruits to experience their products and service firsthand, so they live the experience they are delivering to customers.

Ultimately, you want to create ways to help your team truly understand what the customer experience should look like. Find creative ways to bring the process or product alive so you can build passion and excitement in your employees.

Chapter 10

KNOW ME

I strongly encourage you to consider adding "know me" or some version of the idea to your list of bedrock experience principles. It's an easy concept for people to understand, and it applies to both customer and employee experience. The idea behind this principle is that your people should constantly demonstrate, in big and small ways, that they want to genuinely get to know customers or other employees. When they begin forging those connections, it builds trust, loyalty, and repeat and referral business. The "know me" principle is so important that I would say your experience improvement will be hindered without it.

As a concept, "know me" is about personalization, although not in the traditional marketing sense, where it has become a complicated version of tailoring. Examples of the "know me" principle in practice would be the loyalty programs regularly used by hotel chains and airlines. If you stay at hotels regularly, you're probably already a member of a loyalty program. Early on, they might have sent you a survey about your preferences, with questions such as: Do you prefer a queen- or king-size bed? Do you prefer to stay on a high floor? Do you like to stay near an elevator?

You share your responses to these questions because you hope that a bit of personal information will help the hotel to know you better and make it easier for you to have an enjoyable stay. Sadly, in many instances, when you actually show up to the hotel, your preferences haven't been acted on. Information is collected, but staff don't do anything with it.

Every time a company asks for your preferences and fails to act on them, they are delivering the opposite of the "know me" principle. It's so much harder for customers to feel like they've achieved success if they have to repeat a request for a certain type of pillow or bed every time they check into a hotel. That little bit of extra effort detracts from the overall experience.

It's tempting to think, "But it's only a pillow. Why does it matter?" Perhaps a request for a specific type of pillow doesn't matter much to the customer, but it makes a difference. Small disappointments add up, and they certainly don't contribute to customer loyalty. If you can't meet a customer's request, you should address it. "Mr. So-and-so, unfortunately, we didn't have this type of pillow available, but we thank you for staying at our property."

Too often, companies expend effort to learn about customer preferences and then fail to follow through, so that makes it a great opportunity for your company to differentiate itself.

GETTING TO KNOW YOU

The simplest way to begin demonstrating a willingness to know customers is to learn their names and use them. When someone calls the contact center or walks into a store and introduces themselves, an associate should always use the customer's name—not a colloquial term such as "mate," which might offend some people, but instead their actual name. This might seem like a small thing, but it demonstrates respect, which breeds loyalty.

Learning a customer's name might take a bit of subtle investigative work. When I worked in retail, we trained sales associates, whenever a customer handed them a credit or debit card, to glance at the name before handing it back, then say, "Thank you, Ms. So-and-so." If you've ever stayed at a Ritz-Carlton Hotel, you've probably noticed that by the time you get to the check-in desk, your associate already knows your name. It's almost like magic. You arrive, step out of your car, and the bell service team rushes to grab your bags. Somehow, in the midst of that process, they have learned your name before you even introduce yourself.

How do they do it? The bell service team has a radio and mic. They see your name on your luggage and call ahead to the check-in desk. This allows the associate to locate your portfolio, so they can personalize their greeting. I've stayed at the Marina del Rey Ritz-Carlton a number of times, and whenever I return, they greet me with, "Welcome back to the Marina del Rey Ritz-Carlton, Mr. Bradshaw." They've put a system in place to prepare for a personalized interaction. More than that, this particular hotel has a fantastic team that actually remembers me from previous stays. They're not simply reading information about me from a file. How easy would it be for every hotel to take this simple step? I'm sure in your business you have a similar simple step you could take, so what's holding you back?

You might think that using someone's name is no big deal, but according to an article published by Philip Guo, assistant professor of cognitive science at University of California, San Diego, a person's own name is the single most important word to them.[16] It is, after all, their personal brand's trademark. Due to this deep connection, using a person's name fosters a deeper connection at all moments.

To help with knowing your customers, I recommend investing some time, effort, and perhaps money into a customer relationship management (CRM) system or customer lifecycle management (CLM) system. Essentially, a CLM system combines sales, service, marketing, social media, and ecommerce into a single, or common, platform to allow seamless sharing of data with each internal division, which provides a holistic view of the customer regardless of where they are in the journey.

There's a whole range of CRM systems available, from free platforms such as HubSpot to enterprise-grade systems such as Salesforce. Among these options, you're sure to find one that meets your specific needs. I don't recommend using multiple CRM systems; it's better to have more information in a single repository, which is why I recommend using a CLM system. When you can seamlessly integrate CRM siloed systems, you can more easily connect the dots in a customer's experience to carry out the "know me" experience principle.

---

16   Philip J. Guo, "On Remembering and Dealing with People's Names," PGBovine.net, January 2009, accessed August 14, 2018, http://www.pgbovine.net/on-names.htm.

Consider integrating your CRM or CLM system with Amazon Connect, a SaaS telephone service. When a customer calls, their name and relevant information about their previous interaction appears on the screen, allowing associates to preface the conversation with personalized information such as, "Hello, Ms. So-and-so, are you calling today to follow up on the matter we discussed last time, or can I help you with something else today?"

Most CRM systems can also dynamically route a customer's email inquiry based on the email address it comes from. For example, if you have a particularly sensitive customer segment, you can escalate the speed at which the request is processed and whom it goes to. This kind of tech helps ensure customers receive a level of experience that they appreciate. Companies such as Salesforce and Oracle have advanced integrated solutions that allow you to personalize and customize almost every aspect of an interaction. Based on buying behavior, you can trigger certain marketing messages.

It's all about taking small steps to reinforce to the customer that you want to create a real connection with them.

LEVERAGE CUSTOMER DATA

A great example of a company living the "know me" principle is Tiffany & Co., the global jewelry company.

Everyone loves getting a little blue box from Tiffany's. It's an iconic moment. The company is also inextricably linked to the classic motion picture *Breakfast at Tiffany's*. In fact, they go hand in hand, so visitors to Tiffany's famous Manhattan location will often take a photo of themselves enjoying breakfast in front of the store.

If you look for the company on Twitter, Facebook, or Instagram, you will see numerous pictures of tourists standing in front of Tiffany's while taking a bite out of a croissant, bagel, or other breakfast food. The company's research team realized this and decided to act on it, so they created the Blue Box Café, where visitors can sit and enjoy a full breakfast at the store. This is a great example of knowing your customers and using that information to create a connection with them. It also generated a new revenue stream and arguably another connection point with customers.

Earlier, I mentioned the example of National Australia Bank, which uses a customer's transaction preference to provide a one-button option on their ATMs. For example, if you tend to withdraw $50 from the ATM on weekdays, it might ask, "Would you like to withdraw $50 today?" This "favorite transaction" option was a big step forward in making it easier for customers to achieve success, but ideally, the company shouldn't stop there. You don't want to take a step forward and then stop. Continue looking for ways to make it even easier.

Almost every supermarket chain has some sort of reward program. When a customer goes to the self-service checkout, they can swipe their reward card, cross their fingers, and hope they spent enough to earn the next reward. At the same time, the company tracks shopping behavior and provides personalized offers based on that data. This is a great idea, but I wonder why supermarkets don't take a page out of National Australia Bank's playbook. Why not have the register remember whether a customer typically pays by cash or card and offer them a one-button pay option? Why not even link the rewards card to a preferred payment method so it all happens seamlessly, including emailing the receipt.

Never settle or stop making progress. Even if you've implemented some great ways to remove friction points and build connections, always look for newer and better ways. Getting to know your customers and employees will almost always present you with those better ways.

EMBRACING DIVERSITY

The "know me" principle also applies to your employees, because you should know your team and their intrinsic motivations. This is becoming more important as the workforce and team compositions become more diverse. Just like customer loyalty programs, knowing information about employees doesn't do much good if it doesn't lead to action. I remember a contact center I helped establish in which the company identified the native language of every associate, but they didn't do anything with the information. It just sat in a spreadsheet for twelve months.

We stumbled upon this information while attempting to deal with a customer friction point. Some of the customers who called into the contact center weren't comfortable speaking English because it wasn't their first language. We suggested offering a variety of language options, and that's when the company said, "We created a spreadsheet of languages spoken by our associates twelve months ago."

We dug up the file and used it to start a pilot program in which we connected customers to associates who spoke their native language. This single change led to a huge improvement in post-transactions surveys, they revealed that customers who felt they were treated with dignity and respect, on average, spent more money.

Understanding the diversity of your team members also gives you more ways to celebrate them as individuals. If you have a team member who was born in China, send them a note on Chinese New Year. This shows you're not merely collecting information but getting to know them as people. Of course, you have to do this with a high degree of sensitivity. You don't want to inadvertently promote a negative cultural stereotype in a failed attempt to connect with someone. Still, as organizations become more ethnically diverse, we can embrace and benefit from that diversity.

When is the last time you recognized and celebrated an employee's unique qualities and leveraged that uniqueness to strengthen your connection to them? This applies to far more than ethnicity. One team member might be an avid cyclist; another might volunteer at a local nonprofit. These are all ways you can highlight and celebrate individuals and help them become more successful in the organization.

CONVERSATIONS INSTEAD OF ICEBREAKERS

How many times have you attended a meeting and participated in an icebreaker activity even though, you realized as you looked around the room, at least half the people in the room already knew one another? Maybe you could use your knowledge of individuals to break the status quo and have conversations instead.

How can you expect your team members to be successful at getting to know customers if you don't set the example by getting to know your team members? I challenge you to think of one thing you can do to start creating relationships with new members of your team. Shift them from being employee numbers to being real people with names and unique qualities.

"This is Bob from accounting, and he loves bobsledding."

"This is Marjorie from creative, and she loves bringing numbers to life."

The ultimate challenge in the "know me" principle is to simplify processes and systems so people can get out from behind the bureaucracy to start connecting with the people they interact with on a daily basis.

Chapter 11

CREATE A COMMUNITY OF CEX CHAMPIONS

Have you ever heard the phrase, "If you want to know how to fix something, ask someone on the front line?" There's a lot of wisdom in that saying, but how many organizations systematically create avenues for two-way dialogue with their frontline team members?

The journey of improving customer and employee experience is one of the most challenging that an organization will face because experience is rooted in company culture, and you can't change culture with fancy slogans and posters. To change culture, you have to create *champions*, team members who are truly obsessed with customer and employee experience.

Which of your team members belong to your community

of champions? Start by designating one team member in each team within a department—roughly one champion for every ten to fifteen team members.

The ideal champion is someone who:

1. Is a good communicator
2. Possesses influencing skills
3. Is able to create excitement and commitment
4. Understands and believes in the why for the shift or increased focus on experience
5. Is collaborative but also a challenger-thinker. What's a challenger-thinker? Someone who asks questions such as, "Why can't we improve? Why can't we be better? If we're number one today, why can't we do something to beat ourselves?"
6. Is adaptive
7. Is a team player

The key role of these champions is to create a two-way dialogue between the central experience management team and the wider business to ensure that programs are informed by a wide cross-section of individuals. Also, and most importantly, this ensures that programs are communicated in every team to build understanding, buy-in, and commitment to the ongoing improvement of customer and employee experience.

Choosing members of your community of champions shouldn't be overly complicated. You could choose a champion for each team through a simple team nomination process or through volunteers. Keep the ideal profile of a community champion in mind. You want as many team members as possible to respect and be open to hearing messages and providing feedback to the champion. Start by selecting operational team members, but over time expand to selecting champions from management teams as well.

As an incentive, find ways to provide these champions with access to new development opportunities. I recommend recognizing their contributions during performance reviews.

For a community of champions to work properly, you need to set a few basic ground rules. First, managers must be willing to listen to feedback without getting defensive. Second, champions must be allowed to present ideas in ways that enable change. To do that, you need a facilitator in the community who is responsible for making sure that messaging across the organization, especially upward, is done consistently.

BRINGING THE COMMUNITY TOGETHER FOR RESULTS

The structure of your community of champions depends

on the size of your organization and workgroups. You might be a one-office company, or you might be multi-national. Whatever the case, I encourage you to create individual groups within your community of champions comprised of people from diverse functions within the organization: sales, service, marketing, finance, human resources, and so on. Having a diverse set of individuals in your community provides a diversity of knowledge that can help co-create solutions.

Also, your community doesn't have to meet face-to-face every week (or every month, for that matter), but I would encourage bringing everyone together at least once or twice a year. In-between meetings, use audio and video conferencing tools to connect and create two-way dialogue.

YOUR ORGANIZATION'S TWO COHORTS

Think of your organization as being comprised of two *cohorts*. The first group are the frontline team members who interact with customers the most in their daily roles. This cohort provides the communication to customers. The second cohort is comprised of those people who act as suppliers for the first group. These tend to be removed from customers by one level.

Both must be represented in your community of champions. The idea is to create a balance between customer-focused individuals and those who are removed from customers. Once your two cohorts are identified, bring your champions together and ask them, "What is the biggest roadblock in delivering an experience that builds customer loyalty?"

In the discussion that follows, identify one to three top issues and then, using those same cohorts, workshop ideas to resolve them. Think of this as a "rapid solutions environment" without the expense of hiring consultants. Challenge every suggestion made, and have individual champions challenge one another.

During these meetings, your champions have two primary objectives. First, they need to address systemic problems preventing people from delivering on experience principles. Ask them specific questions around themes that come out of customer and employee research, and make sure every champion has an opportunity to share their ideas and the thoughts of the team they represent. Second, your champions should share what they and their teams are doing to improve experience. Remember, these meetings are designed to collect feedback, not just about problems but also about how teams are employing strategies to make progress.

Have the more experienced champions identify common roadblocks to success throughout the organization.

Some of the problems won't have obvious solutions, but a diverse set of champions is more likely to co-create effective solutions. For example, the problem might be that a rule in the finance department is having a negative impact on other divisions. By having champions from the finance department in the community, it becomes much easier to identify the source of the problem and either modify the rule or ask for a change.

Once everyone agrees to an operational improvement, have your lead champion from both the customer-facing and non-customer-facing cohorts take the idea and present it to key decision makers in order to implement it.

After each meeting, all of your champions can return to their teams and share relevant information with them. This ensures that every individual in the organization knows what's going on. Bear in mind, this doesn't replace the need for other forms of communication. Instead, it acts as reinforcement for what you're already doing, creating another feedback mechanism. In that way, champions become a conduit for important two-way dialogue. This is exactly what it means to become a champion for change.

YOUR PILOT PROGRAM

Obviously, the key to every good idea is implementation.

The best idea in the world does no good if it isn't successfully put into action. So once an operational improvement has been given the green light, you can create a pilot team from both customer- and non-customer-facing cohorts to test the idea. Run an initial test as a catalyst to then share the idea with the C-suite. Ideally, this should be a large enough group of champions to demonstrate the low-cost yet effective company-wide impact of a champions program.

Don't try to champion a massive change like replacing a major IT system. You want ideas that can be rapidly implemented within thirty days or less that will move you closer to your end goals. When you do this, you demonstrate the benefit of having a community of champions, reinforcing your approach while also improving the employee experience in delivering success to customers.

Once you've had some success during the pilot phase, you can replicate what you've done across the company and begin delivering the changes consistently. It's important for companies to see the success that comes from these community actions. It's also important to build momentum, because eventually your community of champions will need to co-create solutions to much bigger problems. When your champions come together for their regular meetings, celebrate the success before identifying new problems.

Just remember the real objective of your community of champions. They should be generating effective two-way communication by sharing the experience transformation journey and actively pulling information from their teams. By having conversations about what's working and not working, you can create feedback for the program. The community of champions should help keep people engaged in the change while also generating interest and excitement for team members.

Another way to create a community of champions is to get employees to use your product. It's the fast track to galvanize your people around making improvements. If you're the leader of a subway system, don't travel to work by car. Take your own subway. If you work in a phone company, use your own phone service.

WHY CHANGE PROGRAMS FAIL

Embedding a culture focused on customer and employee experience is a transformational challenge that requires a long-term commitment to change and continuous improvement. A simple Google search renders heaps of research on why change programs fail. In the *Harvard Business Review* article called "Leading Change: Why Transformation Efforts Fail," author John P. Kotter says that one of the most common mistakes is not creating a powerful enough guiding coalition.[17] I believe your community of champions is that guiding coalition, helping to increase your commitment to customer and employee experience improvement.

You might be familiar with the TV series *Undercover Boss*. I've often wondered how we can take the lessons from that show and immerse our own leaders in the employee experience. On the show, bosses go undercover as frontline employees, and often they are amazed and alarmed at the things happening in their companies. As a result, they introduce significant changes to improve the employee experience. That's fantastic, but how can they scale those changes? I believe a community of champions is a great way to do it.

Sending the boss undercover probably isn't a practical option for you. It also isn't scalable, because there is only one CEO. What can you do to scale immersing the leaders in the real experiences of your employees?

Instead of running an annual employee advocacy survey, why not hold focus groups facilitated by an external agency? Design the focus groups to have employees share their pain points and moments of joy.

---

17   John P. Kotter, "Leading Change: Why Transformation Efforts Fail," Harvard Business Review, January 2007, accessed August 14, 2018, https://hbr.org/2007/01/leading-change-why-transformation-efforts-fail.

If you are a large company, have people managers from another geographical area observe the sessions through a one-way mirror. Make sure the managers don't know the people in the focus group. If you need to go one step further, make sure all the team members have their backs to the mirror so their feedback remains anonymous. In a smaller company, the focus groups can be transcribed to ensure anonymity.

The primary focus of these groups is to humanize the employee experience and offer a wake-up call to managers and leaders in your organization.

After they have heard the feedback, bring your leaders together to workshop the three actions they can implement collectively and consistently in the next ninety days to improve the experience of employees.

This activity will help accelerate the obsession of your people managers to continually improve the experience of your employees.

I have one final question for you. What can you do today to not only get feedback on improving the experience for customers and employees but to also involve your entire organization in co-creating solutions?

CONCLUSION

WHAT'S NEXT?

A little-known fact about me is that I was one of the youngest Tupperware managers in Australia in 2000. Not only was I good at demonstrating and selling the product, but I was also able to help other Tupperware salespeople generate additional income. When I reflect on that time, I realize there's a lot to learn from the planned party industry.

I focused on my Tupperware business only after work and on the weekends, but I earned almost as much selling Tupperware as I did in my forty-hour-a-week job (at the time). The business was entirely dependent on repeat and referral business. Success came from a combination of selling Tupperware at parties and booking additional parties. If I didn't continually book more parties, I didn't get any new customers. The first step in achieving this was making sure my party host achieved success and made connections with guests.

To accomplish this, I had to apply the "know me" principle to understand the goals of my host, so I could help curate a party to achieve those goals. Some hosts knew exactly how many party bookings they wanted to achieve to get the reward they were after. Others, particularly first-time hosts, were sometimes just hoping for a couple of freebies or simply wanted an excuse to get together.

One thing every party had in common was a need for me, as the demonstrator, to make sure my hosts didn't have to expend too much effort. If they had to spend a lot of money on food and time on baking, they wouldn't have the time or energy to encourage friends and guests to also host parties. If their guests thought they had to do a huge amount of work to host a party, they would have been turned off at the idea of doing it themselves. Because I needed party bookings, I focused on making it easy for the host and their guests. That required taking the time to get to know them so I could help each one achieve success.

Because it was a party business, I had to make sure everyone had fun. Of course, I always learned everyone's name. It amazes me how many professionals still don't use real names in their everyday business.

Tupperware is a global company that proves experience is integral to growth and sustainability no matter where you are in the world. If you look at the demonstrators and party hosts who build revenue streams, they do it one relationship at a time.

PEERING INTO THE FUTURE

A question that customer and employee experience professionals often get is, "What is experience going to look like ten years from now?" My reply is, "How would you have answered that question ten years ago, and how close would your answer have been to reality?"

Experiences are judged differently today than they were even three years ago. Don't try to solve problems that might appear a decade from now. Instead, focus on becoming a little bit better today. Rage against indifference. Create a culture that is 100 percent obsessed with customer and employee experience so you're always at least 1 percent better than your key competitors, no matter how expectations evolve over the next ten years.

Your goal is continual improvement, being a little better today than you were yesterday, because a little bit of improvement over time allows you to consistently, systematically, and sustainably deliver on your experience promises. It's much easier to sustain being a little better today than you were yesterday than trying to find and sustain the next greatest idea that will take three years to implement.

TAKE ONE ACTION TODAY

What percentage of your industry's executives would say that customer experience is a top priority? While many CEOs say customer experience is a strategic priority, few customers believe that the companies they do business with are truly committed to the customer experience. As experience professionals, we must change this perception. I challenge you to help set your company apart, to make it famous for delivering an experience that your customers and employees rave about. After all, according to Clarabridge, 45 percent of customers are willing to pay for better customer service.[18]

If you've made it this far in the book, I hope you'll take at least one action today to improve the experience of your customers and employees. Begin building momentum toward delivering an experience at an individual, team, division, or company level that will make you famous. Then maintain a commitment to that experience on a greater scale than organizations have done in the past.

---

18 Lisa Sigler, "19 Fundamental Customer Experience Stats for 2017," Clarabridge. com, January 4, 2017, accessed August 14, 2018, https://www.clarabridge.com/ blog/19-customer-experience-stats-2017/.

Don't waver on that commitment, even if sales figures are slightly off one month. Every organization I've worked with has gone through rough times where the gains of experience transformation slowed down. During those rough times, people often resisted some of the more difficult improvement activities. Don't get discouraged. Don't slow down. Even in hard times, focus on that 1 percent improvement.

As a leader of customer and employee experience, it's important that you find ways to link the work you and your teams do to the commercial health of your organization. When you're faced with the question, "Should we meet our sales target for today or focus on this experience improvement activity?" you should confidently answer, "Today's action to improve experience will directly impact tomorrow's sales by increasing loyalty and repeat business." As you accrue small successes, you will build confidence in that claim, which is why you need to start taking action today.

Write down three actions you plan to take in the next thirty days to improve the experience of your team and three actions you plan to take to improve the experience of the people you and your team serve, whether internal or external customers. I also encourage you to visit www. itsallaboutcex.com and register for additional resources. Modify them to suit your business and your position in transformation, with a view to deliver on that commitment of 1 percent improvement every day.

Look beyond your industry, beyond your discipline, and beyond your country's borders to find inspiration. Learn from what others are doing in other markets and industries to improve the experiences of their customers and employees. Remember, your customers and employees will judge you today based on their latest experience, so start making improvements and change the story.

TEN ACTIONS TO GET STARTED

I have a self-confessed bias for action. Moving forward just 1 percent at a time is worthwhile, in my opinion. I've seen too many great plans fail because of a desire on the part of leaders to achieve perfection before implementation.

Here are ten additional actions everyone can implement to help improve customer and employee experience. They don't have to happen in any particular order, so don't overthink it. Just get started!

- Thank you cards

When was the last time you received a handwritten thank you card? How did it make you feel? It was probably a positive moment, so when was the last time you sent someone a handwritten thank you card?

I'm not the only person to advocate sending personal, handwritten thank you cards. I remember hearing Zig Ziglar talking about this tactic when I was a teenager.

Purchase or print some cards and start sending them to thank employees for a job well done or simply as a sign of appreciation to a customer. The key is to write the card personally.

- Recognition

What have you done in the last week to recognize a team member for doing something amazing? If you start looking for opportunities, you will quickly realize that your team members do amazing things all the time, so take the time to recognize them. After all, behavior rewarded is behavior repeated.

- Talk to customers.

Instead of presenting managers and leaders with decks of information, why not simply get them talking to customers. It is hard for managers and leaders to ignore a human story, even harder when the customer is in front of them (or at the end of the telephone). Connect the real experience with your senior leaders, and they will soon pay greater attention to your efforts to improve experience.

- Put the human back into business.

Stop chasing the score, and start improving the lives of customers and employees. This starts by sharing the stories before the score, putting a face to the experience and making it personal.

- Define your customer and employee promise.

Start defining, revising, and establishing your customer and employee promise.

The Ritz-Carlton does this brilliantly, and it starts with one very simple yet powerful motto: "We are ladies and gentlemen serving ladies and gentlemen." They communicate with clarity their service standards, customer promise (called a credo), and employee promise.

For inspiration, check out their website at www.ritzcarlton.com/en/about/gold-standards#The_Credo.

They publish their standards for all to see and judge them on.

- Get out from underneath your industry.

Stop looking solely at what your industry and competitors are doing, and start exploring what other industries are doing to improve the customer experience. Customers no longer compare their experience with you solely with your competitors. They also judge you based on their experiences in many different industries. To keep moving forward, you need to understand the customer benchmark, regardless of the industry.

- Get stuff done! Put some wins on the board.

Just get started. A child doesn't learn to walk by thinking about it. They learn by doing. They fail, they fall down, but they keep taking steps until they succeed. Your transformation to becoming truly obsessed about customer and employee experience begins when you start taking steps. Success breeds success.

- Make people famous.

Focus on helping to make your team, a colleague, or your boss famous. You read that right. I encourage you to make the people around you famous for delivering amazing customer and employee experiences.

The more people see your programs as contributing

to their success, the more likely they are to be in your corner, to support your requests, and ultimately to help you be successful.

- Read one book a month, and listen to one podcast a week.

When I was a teenager, my parents joined a multilevel marketing (MLM) company. Although my parents were the members, I wound up traveling every month to company meetings and listening to their weekly tapes. Regardless of what you think about MLM companies, I believe the long-term successful businesses such as Amway, Tupperware, and Mary Kay have demonstrated the value of a constant focus on building knowledge and skills. They are the masters of feeding knowledge and inspiration to their members—a focus on continuous learning.

From an early age, I developed a habit of listening to a book on tape every month. Today, I've replaced cassette tapes with podcasts. Here are a few podcasts I listen to regularly: *I Love CX* by Forrester, *Quotable* by Salesforce, *The Chief Customer Officer Human Duct Tape Show* by Jeanne Bliss, *Amazing Business Radio* by Shep Hyken, and *Project Distinct* by Scott McKain. I would also love it if you would subscribe to my own podcast, *It's All about CEX*.

- Be accountable.

A colleague of mine once said, "The standard you walk past is the standard you accept," and I absolutely agree. I believe it starts with the standard you set by example.

At Disney, they call this "stooping to excellence," based on an example set by Walt Disney. Anytime Walt was walking in Disneyland, if he spotted rubbish on the ground (for example), he always stopped to pick it up. The Disney company still encourages this kind of behavior from every cast member, regardless of their job or level.

Hold yourself accountable for establishing the standard in customer and employee experience, then hold others to account as well.

Get started today!

ACKNOWLEDGMENTS

I feel immense gratitude for every organization I've had the opportunity to work with and learn from, and I want to express appreciation for each of the communities I've had the opportunity to give back to.

I offer a sincere thank you to my mother and father, Nicola and David Bradshaw. As an only child, I couldn't have asked for more supportive and encouraging parents, and I know at times they made great sacrifices to help me follow my dreams. I am forever indebted to them.

To my partner and fiancé Ruo Pu Koh: without your support and encouragement, this book would still be sitting on my to-do list. Thank you for everything.

To Michael Bartsch, managing director of Volkswagen Group Australia, I am grateful for your wisdom and guidance.

To the authors who have provided guidance and support during the writing of my first published book, I say, "Thank you."

Finally, to you, the reader, I thank you for buying this book.

ABOUT THE AUTHOR

JASON BRADSHAW created his first business at fourteen, selling telecommunications and computer equipment in the Australian regional city of Toowoomba. In the lead-up to this, he was inspired by books such as *The Pursuit of WOW!* by Tom Peters, which opened his eyes to the power of customer and employee experience.

Jason has tested and implemented strategies for improving experience in a variety of sectors, including telecommunications, retail, media, finance, automotive, health, and not-for-profit. He has worked with companies including Telstra, Target Australia, Fairfax Media, New South Wales Government, Singtel Optus, and Volkswagen Group Australia, and he has sat on the boards of ACON Health Limited and Oz ShowBiz Cares/Equity Fights AIDS.

A cornerstone of Jason's career has been an unwavering commitment to improving the lives of customers and employees. During his time in the telecommunications industry, he was able to implement ideas for improving customer experience in a number of verticals by more than 100 percent. In retail and media, his initiatives to improve efficiencies by focusing on customer and employee experience saved tens of millions of dollars in a matter of months and improved employee retention by double digits year on year.

Jason is currently chief customer officer and director of customer experience at Volkswagen Group Australia. He is also a consultant and regular keynote speaker at business events and conferences.

To contact Jason, visit www.jasonsbradshaw.com.

9 781544 512426